5.

SMP 11-16

Book YX1

CAMBRIDGE
UNIVERSITY PRESS

Published by the Press Syndicate of the University of Cambridge
The Pitt Building, Trumpington Street, Cambridge CB2 1RP
40 West 20th Street, New York, NY 10011–4211, USA
10 Stamford Road, Oakleigh, Melbourne 3166, Australia

© Cambridge University Press 1995

First published 1995

Produced by Gecko Limited, Bicester, Oxon.

Printed in Great Britain by Scotprint Ltd, Musselburgh, Scotland

A catalogue record for this book is available from the British Library

ISBN 0 521 45743 2 paperback

Cover photograph reproduced by permission
of the Trustees of the National Cycle Museum, Lincoln

Contents

1 Angles and circles 1

A Angle in a semi-circle

You need a set-square.

Draw two dots A and B on a piece of plain paper.

A   B
•   •

Use these two dots as guides, so that the sides of the set-square forming the right-angle touch them all the time. What happens to the tip of the 90° angle as you move the set-square about?

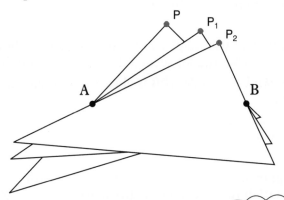

Call the tip of the right-angle P. What is the locus of the point P as it moves from P_1 to P_2, and so on? Describe the locus as accurately as you can.

> A **locus** is the line or path of a set of points which follow a rule.

A1 Turn the set-square over. What is the locus of point P now?

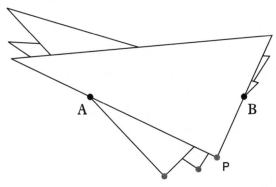

A2 Find the locus of the 45° or 60° tip of your set-square as it moves under the same conditions as the 90° tip above.
Describe the locus in your own words.

You should have found that the locus of the tip of the 90° angle is a circle with AB as diameter.

The locus of each of the other angle tips is an arc of a circle with AB as a chord.

Check to make sure that you agree.

A3 If you drew a circle with centre O and diameter AOB, what value might you expect angle APB to have as P moves round the circle?

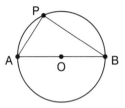

Angle APB is called the **angle in a semi-circle**.

Check your answer by drawing and measuring some angles in a semi-circle for different positions of P.

You probably found that all your angles in a semi-circle were about 90°. Perhaps you found this to be true for several different-sized circles.

Although you might *think* the angle APB is always a right-angle, you have not *proved* it.

You can't say something is true just because it works in a few cases. For all you know they might be special cases.

A4 The diagram shows the same circle as in **A3**, with the line OP drawn and some angles marked.

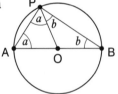

You want to prove that angle APB = $(a + b)$ is always a right-angle, wherever P is on the circle.

Read through this proof before copying and completing the 'because ...' statements.
($\angle$ and $\triangle$ are shorthand for angle and triangle.)

The lines OA, OP and OB are equal because	(a) --------
The angles marked a are equal to each other because	(b) --------
The angles marked b are equal to each other because	(c) --------
In $\triangle$APB, $a + a + b + b = 180°$ because	(d) --------

We can write this as $2(a + b) = 180°$.
So $\angle$APB = $a + b$ = 90°.

We have just proved that:

> The angle in a semi-circle is a right-angle.

A5 Calculate the lettered angles in these diagrams.
All the circles have centre O and diameter AC.
Marks like this ⟩ show sides that are equal in length.

Try to give a reason for each step in your working.

For example, in part (a),

$p = 90° - 55° = 35°$ ($\angle ABC = 90°$, angle in a semi-circle)

(a)

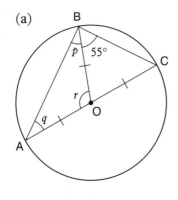

(b)

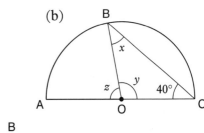

(c)

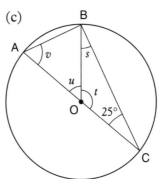

A6 AB is a diameter of a circle with centre O.

(a) If the angle a is 20°, what are the angles b, c and d?

(b) If the angle a is 25°, what are the angles b, c and d?

(c) Work out the size of angle d when angle a is 30°.

(d) Work out d when a is 70°.

(e) Look back at your answers.
What is the relationship between the size of d and the size of a?

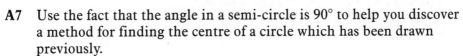

A7 Use the fact that the angle in a semi-circle is 90° to help you discover a method for finding the centre of a circle which has been drawn previously.

Explain your method – a diagram may help.

B Angles on the circumference

The line CB is a diameter of a circle whose centre is O.

A **chord** is the line joining two points on a circle.

The chord AC **subtends** $\angle$AOC at the centre O and $\angle$ABC at the circumference.

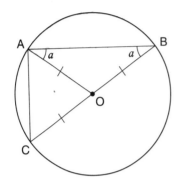

The marks on OA, OB and OC show that they are equal in length (all radii).

$\angle$OAB = $\angle$OBA	(ΔAOB is isosceles)
$\angle$CAB = 90°	(angle in a semi-circle)
$\therefore$ $\angle$CAO = 90° – a	($\therefore$ *means therefore*)
$\therefore$ $\angle$ACO = 90° – a	(ΔACO is isosceles)
$\therefore$ $\angle$AOC = 180° – (90° – a) – (90° – a)	(sum of angles in a triangle)
= 2a	

B1 Try to prove $\angle$AOB is twice the size of $\angle$APB.
Don't forget to give a reason for each step in your working.

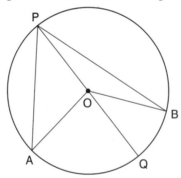

The fact you have just proved is usually stated as:

> The angle at the centre of a circle is twice the angle at the circumference subtended by the same arc or chord.

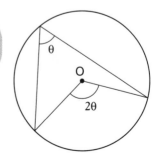

4

B2 Calculate the lettered angles. O is the centre of each circle.
Don't forget to give a reason for each step in your working.

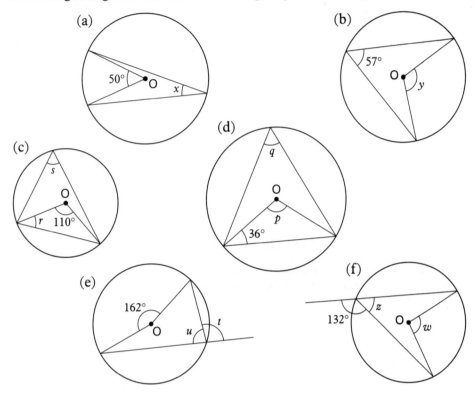

(a)

50°   O   x

(b)

57°   O   y

(c)

s   O   r   110°

(d)

q   O   p   36°

(e)

162°   O   u   t

(f)

132°   z   O   w

B3 This diagram shows a clockface.
[1, 9] means the line joining the points 1 and 9
on the circle.

(a) Calculate the angle between [1, 9] and [1, 4].
Explain how you got your answer.

(b) Calculate the angle between:
(i) [10, 3] and [10, 6]   (ii) [2, 7] and [2, 9]

(c) Investigate the angles between [a, b] and [a, c], where a, b and c are
whole numbers in the range 1 to 12.
Find relationships between these angles and a, b and c.

B4 Explain why the angles marked a and b in
this diagram must be equal to each other.

O is the centre of the circle.

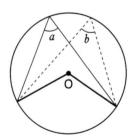

5

This sequence of diagrams shows what happens as the angle at the centre is increased. (The angle at the centre is always twice the angle at the circumference.)

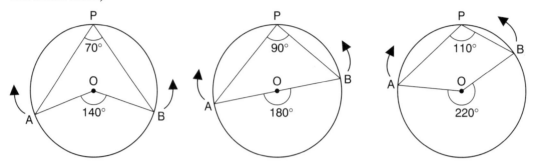

In the third diagram ∠AOB is greater than 180° (it is a **reflex** angle). In this case, the point P is on the shorter arc between A and B.

The other ∠AOB (the non-reflex angle) is 360° – 220° = 140°.

If we join A and B to a point Q on the major (longer) arc AB in this diagram, ∠AQB is half of 140° = 70°.

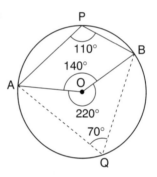

B5 Calculate the lettered angles. O is the centre of each circle.

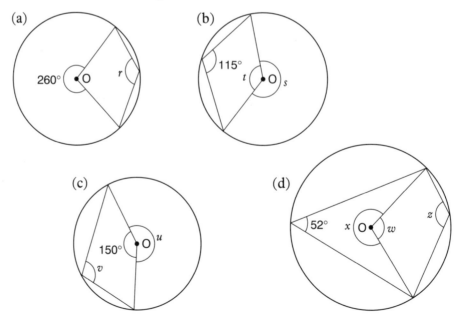

6

Angles at the centre and circumference: a second look and a challenge!

In **B1** you set out to prove that the angle at the centre is twice the angle at the circumference.

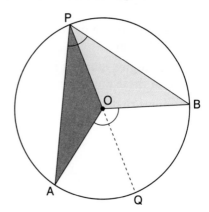

The diameter POQ was drawn and two isosceles triangles made.
In this diagram one is shown dark grey and the other light grey.

But if P were moved until it was quite close to A, some lines would cross over, and the diagram would look like this.

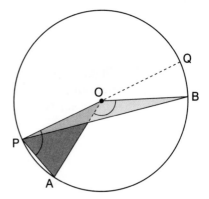

It is still true that ∠AOB is twice ∠APB, but the explanation you probably gave before will not work any more, because the two isosceles triangles overlap one another.

All is not lost! It is still possible to explain why ∠AOB is twice ∠APB.
A larger diagram helps.

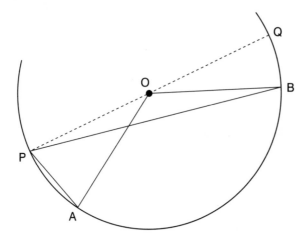

B6 Prove it for yourselves. You may find worksheet YX1–1 useful.
Don't forget to give a reason for each step in your proof.

C Angles in the same segment

A **segment** is the name given to a part of a circle cut off by a straight line.

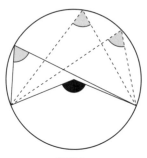

All the angles marked in grey are in the same segment. Each of these angles is half of the angle marked in black.

It follows that the angles marked in grey must be equal to each other.

We have now proved that angles subtended by a chord in a segment are equal.

This is stated briefly as:

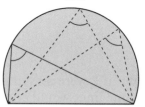

> Angles in the same segment are equal.

C1 There are four pairs of 'angles in the same segment' in the left-hand diagram.
The other two diagrams show two pairs of equal angles.

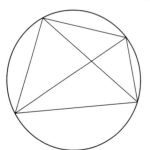
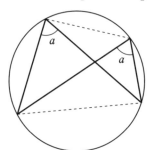
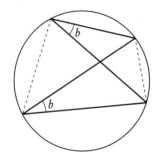

Draw the left-hand diagram. Mark two other pairs of equal angles. Mark one pair c and the other pair d.

C2 Calculate the angles marked p, q, r and s.

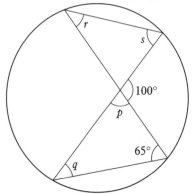

C3 Find the angles marked with letters. The centre of each circle is O.

(a)

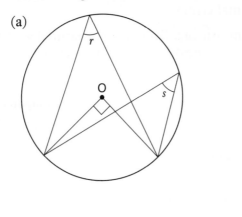

(b)

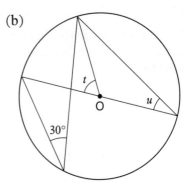

(c)

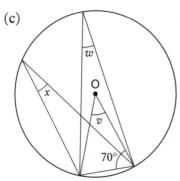

(d)

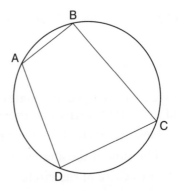

D Cyclic quadrilaterals

A **cyclic quadrilateral** is a quadrilateral whose four vertices (corners) lie on a circle.

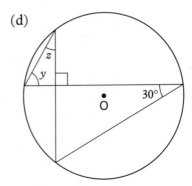

D1 (a) Draw a circle, mark on the circumference four points A, B, C, D, and join them to make a cyclic quadrilateral.

Measure ∠BAD and ∠BCD. What do you notice?
What do you notice about ∠ABC and ∠CDA?

(b) Draw some more cyclic quadrilaterals.
Measure their opposite angles. What do you notice?

You probably found that the opposite angles of your cyclic quadrilaterals added up to 180° (allowing for experimental error).

But you cannot *prove* this just by measuring. Even if you measured a million cyclic quadrilaterals there is always the possibility that it won't be true for the next one!

D2 Draw a cyclic quadrilateral ABCD, together with its diagonals.

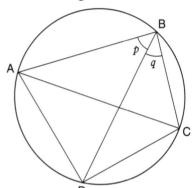

Let p be the size of $\angle$ABD.
Let q be the size of $\angle$DBC.
Mark these on your diagram.

(a) Which other angle must be equal to p? Mark it on your diagram. Why must it be equal to p?

(b) Mark another angle equal to q. Write down the reason why it must be equal to q.

(c) There are two other pairs of equal angles in the diagram. Mark one pair r and the other pair s.

(d) Choose a triangle made by three of the four points A, B, C, D. Use this triangle to explain why $p + q + r + s = 180°$.

(e) Now explain why opposite angles of the quadrilateral add up to 180°.

You have just proved that:

The opposite angles of a cyclic quadrilateral add up to 180°.

In the next two questions you will prove this in other ways.

D3 Prove that the opposite angles of a cyclic quadrilateral add up to 180°, using just these two facts:
(i) Isosceles triangles have a pair of equal angles.
(ii) The sum of the angles of a quadrilateral is 360°.
O is the centre of the circle.

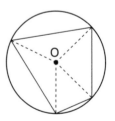

D4 *The angle at the centre of a circle equals twice the angle at the circumference.* Use this fact to prove that the opposite angles of a cyclic quadrilateral add up to 180°.

D5 Find the angles marked with letters.
Don't forget to give a reason for each step in your working.

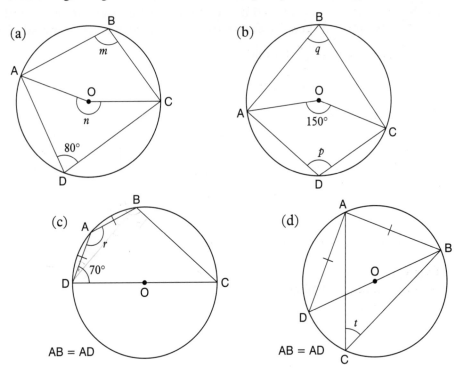

(a)

(b)

(c) AB = AD

(d) AB = AD

D6 What is special about:

(a) a cyclic parallelogram   (b) a cyclic trapezium?

Try to justify your answers to (a) and (b). You could use some of the facts you have met in this chapter.

D7 A cyclic hexagon is a hexagon whose six vertices all lie on a circle.

What is the sum of any three alternate interior angles?

Try to explain your result.

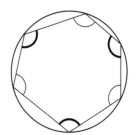

D8 Investigate the properties of quadrilaterals like this. O is the centre of the circle.

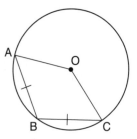

E Deduction

In this chapter we have proved that certain statements about angles and circles are true. We proved them by **deduction**, starting with facts we already knew:

> The angles of a triangle add up to 180°.

> A triangle with two equal sides has two equal angles.

We used these to build up a 'chain' of deductions.

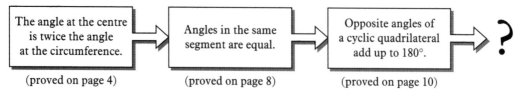

The angle at the centre is twice the angle at the circumference.	Angles in the same segment are equal.	Opposite angles of a cyclic quadrilateral add up to 180°.	?
(proved on page 4)	(proved on page 8)	(proved on page 10)	

We can now use any of these facts to deduce others.

Example
In this diagram, calculate the size of ∠CDE.
Explain each step of your working.

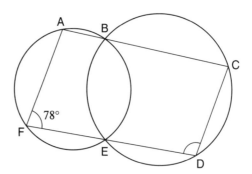

Draw in an extra line BE.
There are now two cyclic quadrilaterals.

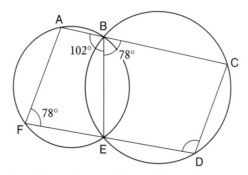

∠ABE = 180° − 78°
      = 102° (opposite angles of a cyclic quadrilateral)
∠EBC = 180° − 102°
      = 78° (angles on a straight line)
∠CDE = 180° − 78°
      = 102° (opposite angles of a cyclic quadrilateral)

E1 Find the sizes of the angles marked with letters.
(O is the centre of each circle.)
Explain your reasons as you go.

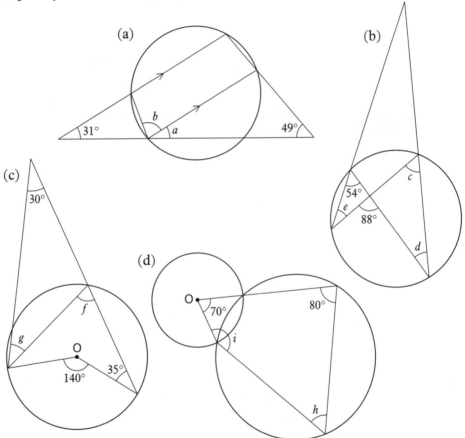

In **E2** and **E3** you will need to make a sketch of the situation before answering. Always check that your drawing fits the information given.

E2 ABCD is a cyclic quadrilateral. Its diagonals intersect at P. ∠BPC = 105°, ∠BAC = 40° and ∠ADB = 30°. Find ∠BCD.

E3 The triangle ABC has its vertices on a circle, centre O. ∠AOB = 90°, ∠AOC = 120°. Find all the angles of the triangle.

E4 The diagram shows a triangle ABC with the side AC extended to D.

∠BCD is an **exterior angle**,

∠BAC and ∠CBA are called its **opposite interior angles**.

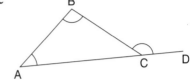

(a) ∠ACB + ∠CBA + ∠BAC = 180°. Why?

(b) ∠ACB + ∠BCD = 180°. Why?

(c) Use the facts in (a) and (b) to explain why
∠BCD = ∠CBA + ∠BAC

You have just shown that:

> The exterior angle of a triangle is equal to the sum of the two opposite interior angles.

This fact can be very helpful. It would, for example, have been useful in **A5** and **A6**. Take a quick look back to see why.

Arcs of circles can be given a 'measure'. One method is to use the angle which the arc subtends at the centre of its circle.

The measure of the arc shown here is ϕ.
(We pronounce ϕ as 'fie'.)

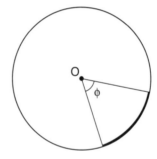

E5 Calculate the 'measure' of each of these arcs. Give a reason for each step in your working.

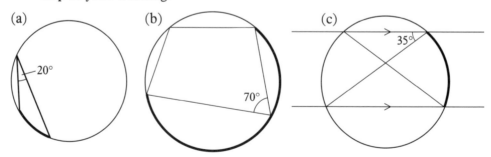

14

E6 This diagram shows a pair of parallel lines cutting a circle at R, S and U, T respectively.

Show that the measure of arc A is equal to the measure of arc B.

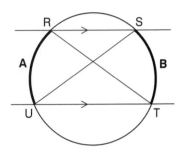

Thinking point

What is wrong with this chain of deduction?

Let two circles intersect at Q and R.
Their diameters are QP and QS.
The line PS cuts the circles at M and N.

∠PNQ and ∠SMQ are right-angles (the angle in a semi-circle is a right-angle).

So QM and QN are both perpendicular to PS.

It looks as if it has just been proved that
there are two perpendiculars from a point to a line!

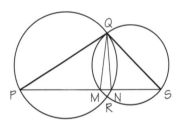

E7 The method described below is used by people sailing small boats.

A and B represent two lighthouses (any two landmarks would do). If there is a hazard inside the circle, the navigator can keep outside the circle if the angle subtended by AB is *less* than the angle ACB.

Explain why the method works.

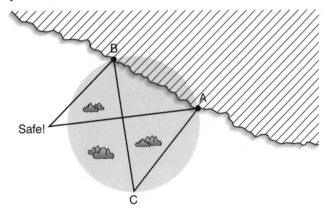

15

E8 A circle has 12 evenly-spaced spots on its circumference. Shapes (including chords) may be made by joining the spots with straight lines.

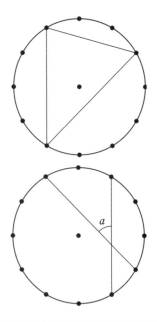

(a) Find out when triangles enclose the centre spot. How does this depend on the angles of the triangle? Try to explain your findings.

(b) Investigate the angles *a* between chords. Don't forget cases where the lines made by chords intersect outside the circle.

(c) Repeat parts (a) and (b) for a 10-point circle.

Summary

- A **chord** is a straight line joining two points on a curve. The line AB is a chord.

  It **subtends** ∠AOB at the centre and ∠APB at the circumference.

  An **arc** is part of the circumference of a circle; the curved lines AB and AP are both arcs.

- The angle subtended at the circumference by a diameter is a right-angle.

- The angle subtended at the centre of a circle is twice the angle subtended at the circumference by the same arc or chord.

- Angles in the same **segment** subtended by an arc or chord are equal.

- A **cyclic quadrilateral** has all four of its vertices lying on a circle. Pairs of opposite angles sum to 180°.

- The **exterior angle** of a triangle equals the sum of the opposite interior angles, that is, ∠SRQ = ∠RPQ + ∠RQP.

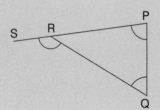

Rooting around ...

The symbols for square root, √ or $\sqrt{\ }$, have been used since the 16th century. Other symbols that have been used are R ($R4 = 2$) and l ($l4 = 2$).

Ancient Indians used their letter for 'c' and the Egyptians the symbol $\lceil$.

On computers, the square root of, say, A, is usually keyed in the form SQR(A).

By convention we assume that when using the √ symbol we are only considering the positive square root or roots – remember $^{-}3 \times {}^{-}3 = 9$ as well!

The root or square root of nine is three.

Thinking point

A very common mistake is to assume that $\sqrt{(a^2 + b^2)} = a + b$.
Are there any values of a and b for which it is true?

The square root of a number may be treated like any other number.

For example, $\dfrac{3}{\sqrt{2}} = \dfrac{3 \times \sqrt{2}}{\sqrt{2} \times \sqrt{2}} = \dfrac{3\sqrt{2}}{2}$

(We write $3 \times \sqrt{2}$ as $3\sqrt{2}$. Also, $\sqrt{2} \times \sqrt{2} = 2$.)

1 Some of these expressions are equal to others. Get rid of the square roots in the denominators to find out which expressions are equivalent.

(a) $\dfrac{2}{\sqrt{3}}$ (b) $\dfrac{6}{\sqrt{2}}$ (c) $\sqrt{3}$ (d) $2\sqrt{3}$ (e) $3\sqrt{2}$ (f) $\dfrac{6}{\sqrt{3}}$

Sometimes different square roots need to be multiplied, for example, $\sqrt{5} \times \sqrt{7}$.
The general rule for this is $\sqrt{a} \times \sqrt{b} = \sqrt{(ab)}$.
This may be proved by squaring both sides.

$$\begin{aligned}
(\sqrt{a} \times \sqrt{b})^2 &= (\sqrt{a} \times \sqrt{b}) \times (\sqrt{a} \times \sqrt{b}) \\
&= (\sqrt{a} \times \sqrt{a}) \times (\sqrt{b} \times \sqrt{b}) \\
&= ab
\end{aligned}$$

But $(\sqrt{(ab)})^2 = ab$, so $\sqrt{a} \times \sqrt{b} = \sqrt{(ab)}$.

This rule is useful in simplifying expressions, for example:

$$\begin{aligned}
\sqrt{300} &= \sqrt{(100 \times 3)} \\
&= \sqrt{100} \times \sqrt{3} = 10\sqrt{3}
\end{aligned}$$

2 Some of these expressions are equal to others. Find out which, by rewriting the square roots of some of them as in the example on page 17.

(a) $\sqrt{8} \times \sqrt{3}$ (b) $\sqrt{12}$ (c) $2\sqrt{6}$
(d) $2\sqrt{3}$ (e) $\sqrt{6} \times \sqrt{2}$ (f) $\sqrt{24}$

3 An approximate value of $\sqrt{2}$ is 1·41.
   Use this to find an approximate value for: (a) $\sqrt{200}$ (b) $\sqrt{8}$

4 Here are the values of some square roots correct to 3 significant figures.

   $\sqrt{2} \approx 1·41$ $\sqrt{3} \approx 1·73$
   $\sqrt{5} \approx 2·24$ $\sqrt{7} \approx 2·65$

   Use these approximate roots to find the values of the following numbers, correct to 2 s.f. You may use a calculator for the multiplication, but only use the square root key to check your answers.

   (a) $\sqrt{6}$ (b) $\sqrt{14}$ (c) $\sqrt{300}$ (d) $\sqrt{7000}$

5 Square root tables enable you to find the square root of any number. There are two sets of tables: square roots from 1 to 10 and square roots from 10 to 100.

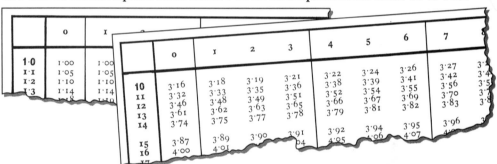

   Explain why only two sets of tables are needed to find the square root of any number.

Thinking point

To calculate the square roots of all whole numbers from, say, 1 to 100, you only need the square roots of all the prime numbers between 1 and 100. Why?

Square roots may also be used in brackets.
Here is an example of multiplying out brackets which contain them.

$(5 + \sqrt{2})(3 - \sqrt{7}) = 15 + 3\sqrt{2} - 5\sqrt{7} - \sqrt{14}$

6 Multiply these out: (a) $(3 + \sqrt{3})(2 + \sqrt{2})$ (b) $(\sqrt{5} - \sqrt{2})^2$

7 Show that these are true:

   (a) $\sqrt{8} + \sqrt{2} = \sqrt{18}$ (b) $\sqrt{8} - \sqrt{2} = \sqrt{2}$ (c) $\sqrt{24} + \sqrt{12} = 2(\sqrt{6} + \sqrt{3})$

2 Rational and irrational numbers

A Changing a fraction to a decimal

Fractions may be changed to decimals by dividing.
Here are two of Stephen's workings.

This shows how he changed $\frac{3}{8}$ into a decimal.

$$\begin{array}{r} 0 \cdot 3\ 7\ 5 \\ \hline 8\ |\ 3 \cdot 0\ \overset{3}{0}\ \overset{6}{0}\ \overset{4}{0} \end{array}$$

$$\frac{3}{8} = 0.375$$

This is how he changed $\frac{2}{7}$ into a decimal.

$$\begin{array}{r} 0 \cdot 2\ 8\ 5\ 7\ 1\ 4\ 2\ 8\ 5\ \ldots \\ \hline 7\ |\ 2 \cdot \overset{2}{0}\ \overset{6}{0}\ \overset{4}{0}\ \overset{5}{0}\ \overset{1}{0}\ \overset{3}{0}\ \overset{2}{0}\ \overset{6}{0}\ \overset{4}{0}\ \overset{5}{0} \end{array}$$

$$\frac{2}{7} = 0.\dot{2}8571\dot{4}$$

Make sure that you understand Stephen's working.

A1 Why do you think he put dots over the 2 and 4?

A2 Use your calculator to change $\frac{2}{7}$ to a decimal.
Why is this answer less accurate than $0 \cdot \dot{2}85\,71\dot{4}$?

Some decimals 'stop' and some 'go on for ever'. Decimals which 'stop' are called
terminating decimals (for example, $0 \cdot 375$). Decimals which 'go on for ever' but
eventually repeat are called **recurring decimals** (for example, $0 \cdot \dot{2}85\,71\dot{4}$).

A3 (a) Change $\frac{7}{11}$ into a decimal without using a calculator.

(b) Change $\frac{4}{7}$ into a decimal without using a calculator.

You should have found that both $\frac{7}{11}$ and $\frac{4}{7}$ start to repeat – some decimals repeat
quicker than others. (If you did not find either of them started to repeat calculate
again, going to more decimal places.)

A4 Change some fractions with denominators less than 15 into decimals
and classify them into recurring or terminating.

How can you predict whether the decimal equivalent of a particular
fraction will recur or terminate?

Investigating recurring decimals without the aid of a computer can be very tedious. A calculator can help, but many calculators display 10 digits at most and $\frac{1}{113}$, for example, repeats in 112 digits!

Here are two pieces of coding: one a spreadsheet, the other in BASIC. Both calculate the decimal equivalent of a fraction, but are in an incomplete form. For example, neither gives the position of the decimal point and the BASIC coding does not print out the results very neatly. You may wish to choose one and improve the coding. Alternatively, you could use a programmable calculator to write a program of your own. (The BASIC coding might help.)

	A	B	C	D	E
1	17				
2	A1 stores denominator		0	0	0
3	Numerator	1			
4	Number to be divided	=B3	=10*B7+C3	=10*C7+D3	=10*D7+E3
5	Result of division	=B4/$A1	=C4/$A1	=D4/$A1	=E4/$A1
6	Whole number answer	=INT(B5)	=INT(C5)	=INT(D5)	=INT(E5)
7	Remainder	=B4-B6*$A1	=C4-C6*$A1	=D4-D6*$A1	=E4-E6*$A1
8	Answer	=B6	=C6	=D6	=E6

	A	B	C	D	E
1	17				
2	A1 stores denominator				
3	Numerator	1	0	0	0
4	Number to be divided	1	10	100	150
5	Result of division	0.058824	0.588235	5.882353	8.823529
6	Whole number answer	0	0	5	8
7	Remainder	1	10	15	14
8	Answer	0	0	5	8

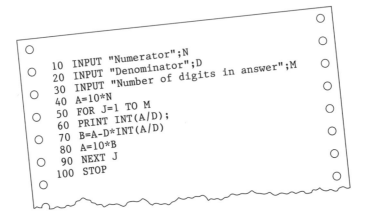

```
10  INPUT "Numerator";N
20  INPUT "Denominator";D
30  INPUT "Number of digits in answer";M
40  A=10*N
50  FOR J=1 TO M
60  PRINT INT(A/D);
70  B=A-D*INT(A/D)
80  A=10*B
90  NEXT J
100 STOP
```

The first 21 steps in the calculation for $\frac{1}{17}$ are:

$$0 \cdot 0\ 5\ 8\ 8\ 2\ 3\ 5\ 2\ 9\ 4\ 1\ 1\ 7\ 6\ 4\ 7\ 0\ 5\ 8\ 8$$

$$17\ \big|\ 1 \cdot \overset{1}{0}\ \overset{10}{0}\ \overset{15}{0}\ \overset{14}{0}\ \overset{4}{0}\ \overset{6}{0}\ \overset{9}{0}\ \overset{5}{0}\ \overset{16}{0}\ \overset{7}{0}\ \overset{2}{0}\ \overset{3}{0}\ \overset{13}{0}\ \overset{11}{0}\ \overset{8}{0}\ \overset{12}{0}\ \overset{1}{0}\ \overset{10}{0}\ \overset{15}{0}\ \overset{14}{0}$$

The remainders go 1, 10, 15, 14, 4, 6, 9, 5, 16, 7, 2, 3, 13, 11, 8, 12,
and then repeat.

This calculation goes through every possible remainder from 1 to 16, so there
are 16 recurring figures in the decimal. (There cannot be more than 16,
because there are only 16 different possible remainders.)

A5 Look back at the paragraph above. Explain why, once a remainder
is repeated, the decimal has started to recur.

A6 Work out the decimal for $\frac{1}{13}$. Does it have the maximum possible
number of recurring figures?

A7 Do all decimal equivalents of fractions which 'go on for ever'
eventually repeat? Investigate. Explain your findings by looking
at the remainders.

⬤ *Thinking point* ─────────────────────────────

In the calculation of $\frac{2}{17}$, the first remainder is 2 and the second 3.

Eddie says, without doing any calculation, that the next two remainders are
13 and 11. How did Eddie know this?

◼ *Options* ─────────────────────────────

- List the integers (whole numbers) from 1 to 50 whose reciprocals give
  (i) terminating decimals,
  (ii) decimals, recurring in blocks of 1, 2, 3 digits.
- Investigate the order of the recurring digits in the decimal equivalents of
  $\frac{1}{7}, \frac{2}{7}, \frac{3}{7}, \dots$
  What about $\frac{1}{17}, \frac{2}{17}, \frac{3}{17}, \dots$?

B Changing decimals into fractions.

Terminating decimals are easily changed to fractions.

For example, $0.6 = \dfrac{6}{10} = \dfrac{3}{5}$

$0.63 = \dfrac{63}{100}$

and $0.635 = \dfrac{635}{1000} = \dfrac{127}{200}$

B1 Change these decimals to fractions.

(a) 0.85 (b) 0.408 (c) 0.0256 (d) 0.0125

Recurring decimals can also be changed into fractions.

Example Change $0.\dot{4}\dot{7}$ into a fraction.

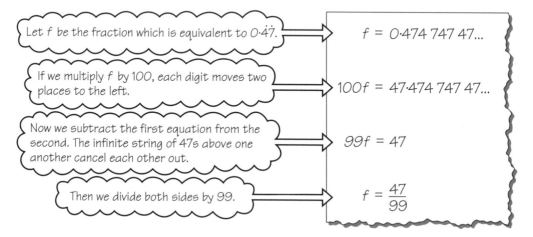

Let f be the fraction which is equivalent to $0.\dot{4}\dot{7}$.

$f = 0.474\ 747\ 47...$

If we multiply f by 100, each digit moves two places to the left.

$100f = 47.474\ 747\ 47...$

Now we subtract the first equation from the second. The infinite string of 47s above one another cancel each other out.

$99f = 47$

Then we divide both sides by 99.

$f = \dfrac{47}{99}$

B2 Use or adapt the method above to change each of these into a fraction. Simplify your fractions if necessary.

(a) $0.\dot{2}\dot{3}$ (b) $0.\dot{5}$ (c) $0.3\dot{8}\dot{4}$ (d) $0.4\dot{5}$ (e) $0.\dot{1}4\dot{8}$

Check your answers by changing them into decimals using a calculator.

B3 Adapt the method above to change each of these into a fraction.

(a) $0.4\dot{7}$ (b) $0.7\dot{2}\dot{1}$ (c) $0.346\ 1\dot{5}$

Check your answers.

B4 Investigate the decimal equivalents of fractions whose denominators are 999.

C Irrational numbers

We use the term **rational number** to describe all numbers which can be written in the form $\frac{a}{b}$ where a and b are integers. (b cannot be zero.)

So $\frac{2}{3}$, $\frac{7}{4}$, $\frac{7643}{72\,931}$, $43\,(=\frac{43}{1})$ and $2\cdot12\,(=\frac{212}{100})$ are all rational numbers.

The word 'rational' is related to the word 'ratio'.

- Every terminating or recurring decimal is a rational number.
- The decimal equivalent of every rational number either terminates or recurs.

The term **irrational number** describes a number which is not rational.

Two examples of irrational numbers are $\sqrt{2}$ and π. The Ancient Greeks could prove that $\sqrt{2}$ is irrational over 2000 years ago, but it was not until the 18th century that π was proved to be irrational.

Although $\sqrt{2}$ and π cannot be written exactly as decimals, we can calculate them as accurately as we need. For example $\sqrt{2}$, correct to 40 significant figures, is:

   1·414 213 562 373 095 048 801 688 724 209 698 078 570

and π to the same accuracy is:

   3·141 592 653 589 793 238 462 643 383 279 502 884 197

Values of π have been calculated to several million significant figures, but so far no pattern has been found in the digits. However, some patterns which occur by pure chance have been observed. For example, there are six consecutive 9s between decimal places 762 and 767, but the sequence of digits 123456789 has not yet been observed!

C1 A sequence of increasingly better approximations to $\sqrt{2}$ is

$$\frac{1}{1}\quad \frac{3}{2}\quad \frac{7}{5}\quad \frac{17}{12}\quad \frac{41}{29}\quad \frac{99}{70}\quad \ldots$$

If one term is $\frac{a}{b}$, the next is $\dfrac{a+2b}{a+b}$.

Find the next two terms in the sequence.

As an approximation to $\sqrt{2}$, how accurate (i.e. to how many decimal places) is the eighth term of the sequence?

C2 The terms having an odd denominator in the sequence in **C1** have this curious property.

> The sum of the squares of the two consecutive numbers which sum to the numerator is equal to the denominator squared.

Show that this is true for some of the terms in the sequence.

We will now look at some proofs that $\sqrt{2}$ is irrational. The method used is called **proof by contradiction**.

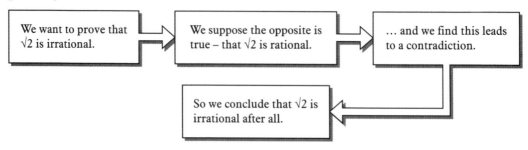

A proof that $\sqrt{2}$ is irrational

Assume that $\sqrt{2}$ is rational. This means that we can write

$$\sqrt{2} = \frac{a}{b}, \text{ where } \frac{a}{b} \text{ is as simple as possible.}$$

So $2b^2 = a^2$ (squaring both sides and multiplying by b^2)

As the fraction $\frac{a}{b}$ is as simple as possible, a and b do not share any factors. (If this were not true, a and b could both be divided by these factors giving a simpler fraction.)

When a number is squared, its units digit can only be a 0, 1, 4, 5, 6 or 9.

C3 Explain in your own words why this is true.

This means that both a^2 and b^2 may only end in a 0, 1, 4, 5, 6 or 9.
But a^2, because it is equal to $2b^2$, may only end in a 0, 2 or 8.
So a^2 can only end in a zero and b^2 $(=\frac{1}{2}a^2)$ can only end in a zero or 5.
So a can only end in zero and b in a zero or 5.

If this is true, it means that 5 divides into both a and b.
But this contradicts the starting assumption that a and b have no factors in common.

So the assumption that $\sqrt{2}$ is rational is contradicted.

Another proof that $\sqrt{2}$ is irrational

This proof is based on what is sometimes called the Fundamental Theorem of Arithmetic.

> 'Every whole number can be made from the product of one, and only one, set of primes. It has its own *unique* set of prime factors. For example, $12 = 2 \times 2 \times 3$ ($2 \times 3 \times 2$ does not count as different). There is no other set of primes whose product is 12.'
>
> This means that as $12 = 2 \times 2 \times 3$, and $15 = 3 \times 5$, then
> $$12 \times 15 \,(= 180) = 2 \times 2 \times 3 \times 3 \times 5.$$
> So if a number a has, say, 5 prime factors and another number b has 7 prime factors, the number ab, the product of a and b, will have $5 + 7 = 12$ prime factors. If you are not quite sure of this, work through with some numbers of your own.
>
> A prime number has just one prime factor – itself!

We can now begin the proof.
As before, assume that $\sqrt{2}$ is rational, so that $a^2 = 2b^2$.

- If a has n prime factors, a^2 will have $2n$. This means that:
  a^2 has an even number of prime factors.

- For the same reason, b^2 must also have an even number of prime factors.

- '2' has only one prime factor,
  so $2b^2$ must have an odd number of prime factors.

- We have a *contradiction* because a number cannot have both an even number of prime factors *and* an odd number.

- So the starting assumption must be wrong and $\sqrt{2}$ must be irrational.

A proof that $\sqrt{2}$ is not a terminating decimal with three decimal places

Assume that $\sqrt{2}$ is a terminating decimal with three decimal places.
If this is so, then $\sqrt{2} = 1{\cdot}abc$, and c must be non-zero.
(a, b and c are single digits like the 6, 3 and 9 in 639. Here abc does *not* mean a × b × c.)

- $\sqrt{2} = 1{\cdot}abc$ can be written as $\qquad \sqrt{2} = 1 + \dfrac{abc}{1000}$
  $$\text{or } 1000\sqrt{2} = 1000 + abc$$

- Squaring each side gives $2\,000\,000 = (1000 + abc)^2$

- This is a *contradiction* because the units digit on the left-hand side is *zero*, but as c is non-zero the units digit on the right-hand side is *non-zero*. So the starting assumption must be wrong.

  Therefore $\sqrt{2} = 1{\cdot}abc$ is not true, so $\sqrt{2}$ is not a terminating decimal with three decimal places.

- We can extend this proof to 1, 2, 4, 5, ... decimal places.

C4 Choose at least two of the proofs and adapt them to prove that each of these are irrational numbers.

(a) $\sqrt{3}$ (b) $\sqrt{7}$ (c) $\sqrt{8}$ (d) $\sqrt{22}$

Challenge

Prove that the square root of any prime number is irrational.

C5 One of these lines has a gradient of $\frac{1}{2}$, the other a gradient of $\frac{1}{3}$.

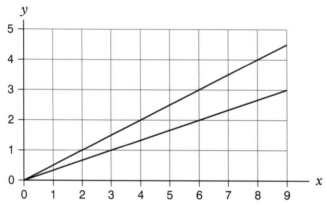

If you look carefully at the two lines you will see that they each go through grid line intersections several times.

Does this happen with lines whose gradients are:

(a) $\frac{2}{3}$ (b) $\sqrt{\frac{1}{4}}$ (c) 2   (d) $\sqrt{2}$ (e) $\sqrt{\frac{1}{2}}$?

Give reasons for your answers.

Thinking point

Are these true or false? Give reasons and examples to support your answers.

- The product of two irrational numbers is also irrational.
- Although you cannot write down in figures an irrational number exactly, you can draw a line whose length is an irrational number (for example, a line $\sqrt{2}$ units long).
- Squares of irrational numbers are always irrational.
- Multiplying an irrational number by a whole number can give a rational number.
- Adding together a rational and an irrational number can sometimes give a number which is rational.

For calculations involving irrational numbers, it can sometimes help to use rational approximations. Here is a method of finding, for example, a rational approximation to √2. A similar method was used by the Ancient Greeks.

√2 ≈ 1·414 (One, not very helpful, answer would be $1 + \frac{414}{1000}$.)

Let √2 ≈ $1 + \frac{1}{a}$ where a is an integer.

So a = the whole number part of $(1·414 - 1)^{-1}$

$\quad (0·414)^{-1} = 2·415\,458 \ldots$

$\quad\quad \therefore a = 2$

This means that a better approximation for √2 is $1 + \frac{1}{2} + \frac{1}{b}$ where b is an integer.

By a similar method to that used to find a, b is given by the whole number part of:

$\quad (1·414 - 1·5)^{-1} = {}^-11·627 \ldots$

So the improved rational approximation to √2 is given by:

$\quad 1 + \frac{1}{2} - \frac{1}{11}$, which is equivalent to $\frac{31}{22}$.

A closer approximation can be found by repeating the process above.

C6 (a) Using the method above, what is the simplest rational approximation, involving fractions, to π? (Take π = 3·1416.)

(b) How does your rational approximation help you, when finding the area of a circle of radius 7 metres?
(Before calculators were widely used, maths textbooks always had circles with radii as multiples of 7!)

C7 Use the method above to find a rational approximation to √10.
(Use the value of √10 correct to 3 significant figures.)

Summary

- A **rational number** is one which can be expressed as a fraction.
  $27(\frac{27}{1})$, $1·25 (\frac{125}{100})$ and $0·75 (\frac{3}{4})$ are rational numbers.

- An **irrational number** is one which cannot be written as a fraction.
  √2, √5, π and 2√2 are all irrational numbers.

- Changing fractions into decimals can result in one of two types of decimal: **terminating** (0·25) or **recurring** (0·573 573 573 ... which is written as 0·5̇73̇).

- It is always possible to find the fraction which gives a particular recurring decimal.

- In a **proof by contradiction** something is assumed to be true and deductions made based on this. These deductions are then shown to be false, so contradicting the original assumption. The original assumption must therefore be false.

3 Tangents and curves

A Gradients and straight lines – a review

The **general equation** of a straight line is $y = ax + b$.

The straight line has **gradient** a and **y-intercept** b.

So the graph here, whose equation is $y = 2x - 1$, has gradient 2 and y-intercept ⁻1.

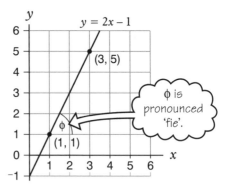

φ is pronounced 'fie'.

A1 Ayesha suggests that the gradient of this line, which can be found by working out, $\dfrac{5-1}{3-1} = 2$ for example, is the same as the tangent of φ, the angle the line makes with the x-axis. Is this generally true?

A2 Draw some pairs of straight lines which cut each other at right-angles. What is the connection between their gradients? (You may find using a graph-plotting device useful.)

A3 For the line $y = ax + b$, find a connection between the gradient a, the y-intercept b and the x-intercept c.

Write down the general equation for a straight line, which only involves the x- and y-intercepts, b and c.

A4 A general expression for finding the gradient of a line joining the two points (x_1, y_1) and (x_2, y_2) is $\dfrac{y_2 - y_1}{x_2 - x_1}$.

Show that the rule works for:

(a) all situations where $x_2 < x_1$

(b) all situations where $y_2 < y_1$

Imagine the straight line $y = 2x + 4$ and a point, for example (1, 6) on this line. If the x-coordinate is increased by 1, then the change in the y-coordinate is 2.

The change in the y-coordinate when the x-coordinate is increased by 1 is the same for any point on the line. It is called the **rate of change of y with respect to x** for points on the straight line.

A5 Describe carefully, with reasons, the connection between the rate of change of y with respect to x on a straight line and the gradient.

A6 Try to answer this question without drawing an accurate graph – just make a rough sketch if necessary.

There are five points A $(2, ^-5)$, B $(4, 3)$, C $(^-10, 8)$, D $(^-6, ^-5)$ and E $(5, 0)$. The straight lines AB, AC, AD and AE are drawn.

(a) Which of these lines have (i) zero gradient, (ii) positive gradient, (iii) negative gradient?

(b) Calculate the gradients of AB, AC, AD and AE.

A7 Calculate the rate of change of temperature for the straight line segments of these graphs. Don't forget to give the units of the gradient – a temperature rise of 1°C per second is a different rate of change to one of 1°C per year!

(a)

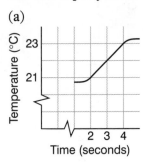

(b)

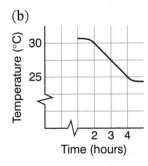

(c)

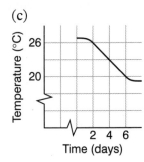

A8 Here are the sketches of some graphs. For each one write down the units of the gradient and, where possible, what the gradient means. In some cases the gradient may have a common name.

(a)

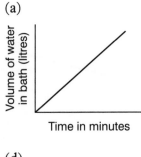

(b)

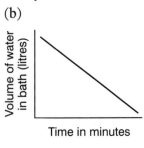

(c)

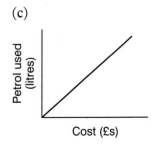

(d)

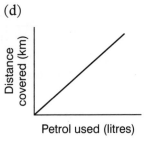

(e)

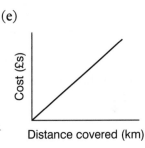

(f)

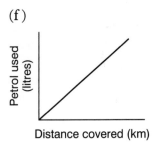

B   The gradient of a curve

In this heating experiment, the graph of
temperature against time is a curve.
The rate of change of temperature against
time is not constant – it changes with time.

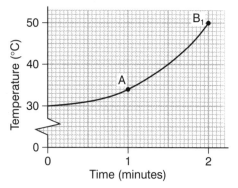

We can only calculate the *average* rate of change of temperature, which is the
change in temperature divided by this time interval.

For example, during the second minute
(between $t = 1$ and $t = 2$ minutes), the
average rate of change is equal to the
gradient of line AB_1

$$= \frac{50 - 34}{2 - 1}$$

$$= 16\,°C \text{ per minute}$$

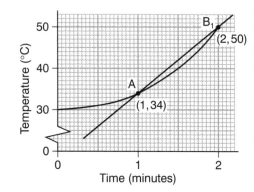

B1 Calculate the average rate of change of temperature between $t = 1$ and
$t = 1\cdot5$ minutes if, during this time, the temperature changes from
$34\,°C$ to $40\,°C$.

B2 This is an enlargement of the graph at around 1 minute.

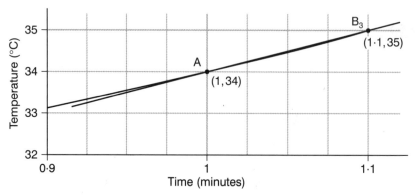

Use it to calculate the average rate of change of temperature between
$t = 1$ and $t = 1\cdot1$ minutes.

This graph summarises the average rates that have been calculated.

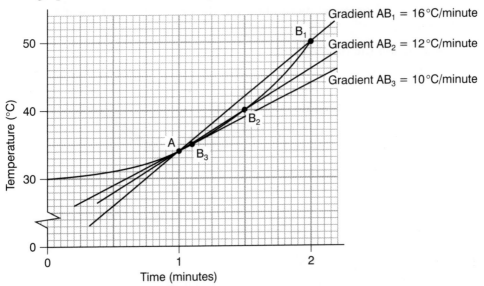

Gradient $AB_1 = 16\,°C/minute$

Gradient $AB_2 = 12\,°C/minute$

Gradient $AB_3 = 10\,°C/minute$

The gradients of the **chords** (a chord is a line that cuts a curve in two places) AB_1, AB_2 and AB_3 give the average rate of change of temperature over smaller and smaller time intervals from 1 minute.

As the point B moves closer and closer to A, the straight line containing A and B will approach the straight line which *touches* the curve at A.

This is called the **tangent** to the curve at A.

It is the only line that touches at A.

The gradient of the tangent line is called the **gradient of the curve at point A**.

This gradient also gives the **rate of change** of the temperature at $t = 1$ minute.

To measure this gradient, we need to draw the tangent line.
It is difficult to construct this exactly (unless the curve is the arc of a circle) but we can estimate it.

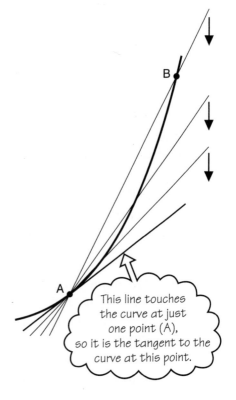

This line touches the curve at just one point (A), so it is the tangent to the curve at this point.

B3 You need worksheet YX1–2 and a transparent ruler.

Here is one practical method to find the gradient of a curve at a point A.

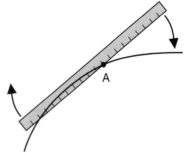

- Position the ruler over the point A.

- Rotate the ruler until its edge just touches the graph at A. Now draw this line, which is the tangent at A.

- Use graph paper to calculate the gradient of the line at A.

(a) Write down the rate of change of the temperature at 1 minute.

(b) By drawing tangents, find the rate of change of the temperature at:
 (i) 2 minutes, (ii) 0·5 minutes.

B4 You need worksheet YX1–3.

This shows a graph of the height above mean sea-level, on a certain day at Liverpool docks, against hours after midnight.

Find: (a) the rate at which the height is increasing at 02:00,

(b) the rate at which the height is decreasing at 06:00.

Options

- How consistent is the 'plastic ruler method' described above in finding gradients of curves? Experiment – gather some data.

- Can you find any other practical method of finding the gradient at a point? (Perhaps you had to do this in science.)

Test your method. Is it more consistent than the method involving the rotation of a transparent ruler?

B5 On graph paper draw a set of axes, with y from 0 to 10 in 2 cm units and x from $^-3$ to 3 in 2 cm units.

Plot the values (x, y) for $y = x^2$. Use sufficient points to draw a smooth curve.

Measure the gradient of the curve at each of the points $x = ^-2, ^-1, 0, 1, 2$.

Can you find a connection between the x-coordinate and the gradient at that point? Check your result by finding the gradient at some more points.

If you know the equation of a curve, a graph-plotting device can be used.

B6 Here are the graphs of $y = x^2$ and $y = x$.
The grid scales have been increased in going from diagram 1 to 4.
This is sometimes called 'zooming in'.

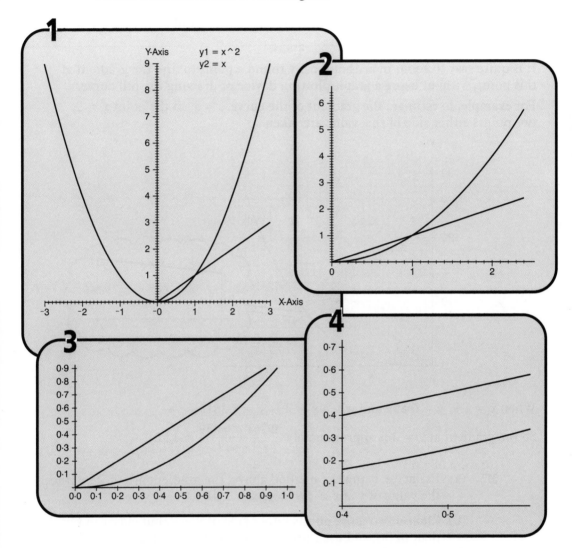

(a) What appears to happen to the curve $y = x^2$ as the scales are
increased (or you zoom in)?

(b) Explain how you could estimate the gradient of $y = x^2$ at $x = 0.5$
from the zoomed-in pictures.

(c) Explain how you *could* use a graph-plotting device (a graphical
calculator or graph/function drawing program) to find the gradient
of the curve $y = x^2$ at the point $x = 1$.

- Use a graph-plotting device to check your answers to **B5**.

- Investigate gradients on the graph $y = \dfrac{x^3}{3}$, for $x = {}^-2, {}^-1, 0, 1, 2$.

  Can you find a relationship between the gradient and x?

It is quite easy to zoom in arithmetically round a point to find the gradient at this point, without using a graph-plotting device or drawing the full curve.

For example, to estimate the gradient of the curve $y = x^3$ at the point $x = 2$, two points either side of this value are taken.

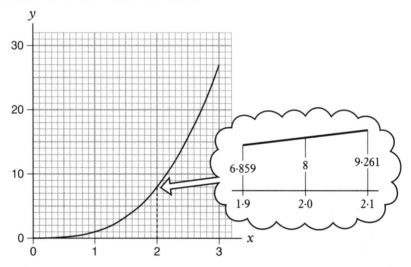

When $x = 1 \cdot 9$, $y = 6 \cdot 859$ and when $x = 2 \cdot 1$, $y = 9 \cdot 261$.

So the gradient at $x = 2$ is approximately $\dfrac{9 \cdot 261 - 6 \cdot 859}{2 \cdot 1 - 1 \cdot 9} = 12 \cdot 01$.

B7 (a) Estimate, using the method above, the gradient at $x = 2$ by finding the value of y at $x = 1 \cdot 99$ and $x = 2 \cdot 01$.

(b) Choose two more points either side of $x = 2$, but closer to $x = 2$ than in (a), and use these to make another estimate.

(c) What do you notice about your answers to (a) and (b)?

B8 Use the method above to find the gradient of the curve $y = x^2$ at each of the points $x = 1, 1 \cdot 5, 2$ and $2 \cdot 5$. Try to spot a pattern.

B9 Repeat **B8** for some curves of your own, for example $y = x^2 + 3x$ and $y = \dfrac{1}{x}$. In each case, find the gradient at four or five points and try to spot a pattern.

c Using gradients

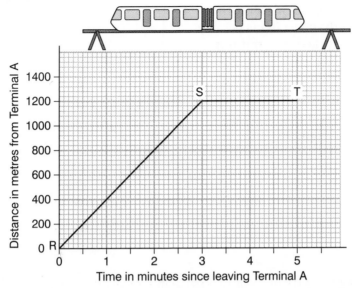

This graph shows the journey of an airport shuttle travelling from Terminal A to Terminal B, a distance of 1200 metres.

C1 Use the distance–time graph to answer these questions.

(a) What is the gradient of the line RS? Don't forget the units!

(b) What does the gradient of RS represent?

(c) The gradient of the line ST is zero. What does this tell you?

(d) Five minutes after leaving Terminal A the shuttle leaves Terminal B for the return journey. The return journey takes two minutes.

Copy the graph above and add to it this return journey.

C2 Why is it very unlikely that the real distance–time graph will be made up of straight line segments? Make a sketch showing what you might expect the real graph to look like.

Gradients of graphs (including the sign) usually have a meaning. If you are not quite sure what it is or want to check, looking at its units may be helpful.

For example, this graph shows the voltage applied to a resistor for different values of the current passing through it in amps. The units of the gradient are

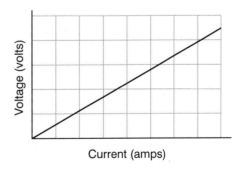

$$\frac{\text{volts}}{\text{amps}} \text{ or volts per amp.}$$

This is called the resistance.

Curves with a shape like this are sometimes called learning curves.

Imagine that the *y*-axis represents the number of correctly-made items per day and the *x*-axis the practice or training time. Then the curve gives a sensible idea of how long someone takes to learn how to do a job.

It could also represent the total sales of a car or CD, for example.

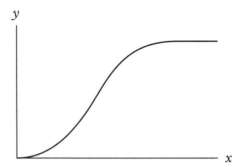

C3 Describe how the gradient of a learning curve changes.
Can you think of any other situations which give a learning-type curve?

Velocity
Velocity is a measure of *speed* in a particular *direction*.

For example, a car travelling north whose *speed* is 50 m/s has a *velocity* of 50 m/s *due north*.

In this chapter, all the objects are moving in a straight line (along a straight track, or vertically upwards in the case of a rocket), so that when we talk about speed in this direction, we do in fact mean velocity.

Acceleration is the rate of change of velocity.

C4 You need worksheet YX1–4. The graph shows how the height of a rocket launched vertically changes with time.

(a) By drawing tangents to the graph, find the velocity of the rocket at these times after lift-off:
(i) 1 second (ii) 3 seconds (iii) 5 seconds

(b) Try to describe in your own words the part of the rocket flight represented by the graph.

C5 You may have seen adverts like this.

(a) What is the average acceleration of this car?

(b) One of the largest accelerations recorded by a production car was 0–160 km/h in 9·8 seconds. What acceleration is this?

C6 You need worksheet YX1–5. The graph shows how the velocity of a small, vertically-launched rocket changed with time.

(a) What is the acceleration 2 seconds after lift-off?

(b) What is the maximum acceleration of the rocket during the first 7 seconds after lift-off?

Thinking point

Mark says that a graph showing the forward velocity against time of an aircraft coming in to land has the same shape as the actual path taken by the plane.

Cheryl disagrees and says that it is the graph of the plane's distance from the control tower against time which gives this path.

Who, if either, is correct? Explain your answer carefully.

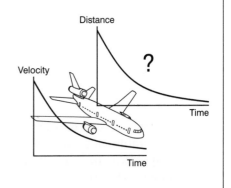

Summary

- A **tangent** is a straight line that touches a curve at just one point.

- The gradient of a line on a graph gives the **rate of change** of the *y*-value for a given change in the *x*-value.

  The rate of change of distance with time (on a distance–time graph) gives the velocity.

  The rate of change of velocity with time gives the acceleration.

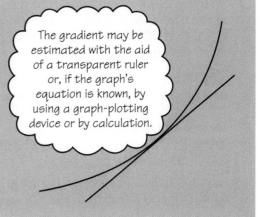

The gradient may be estimated with the aid of a transparent ruler or, if the graph's equation is known, by using a graph-plotting device or by calculation.

Too soon to calculate ...

Marion had to find the length of x in this diagram.

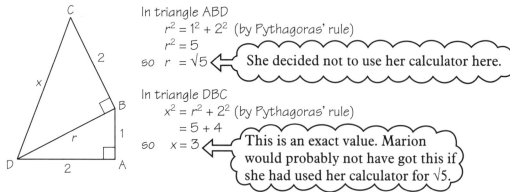

In triangle ABD
$$r^2 = 1^2 + 2^2 \text{ (by Pythagoras' rule)}$$
$$r^2 = 5$$
so $r = \sqrt{5}$ ← She decided not to use her calculator here.

In triangle DBC
$$x^2 = r^2 + 2^2 \text{ (by Pythagoras' rule)}$$
$$= 5 + 4$$
so $x = 3$ ← This is an exact value. Marion would probably not have got this if she had used her calculator for $\sqrt{5}$.

It is sometimes easier to 'carry round' an expression in a calculation without finding its value on a calculator. For example, $\sqrt{5}$ is a lot easier to write down than its approximate value by calculator, which is 2·236 067 977! Also, there may be the chance that the 'exact' value will give an exact final answer.

Leaving the actual calculation as late as possible may have the advantage that your working is lot easier to follow.

1 Without using a calculator, find the lengths of the lines OA, OB, OC, ... (The angles OXA, OAB, OBC, ... are all right-angles.) What do you notice?

The lines joining up the points A, B, C, ... make a shape called an Archimedean spiral.

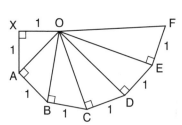

2 Here is another spiral-like shape. Try to find a pattern in the lengths OA, OB, OC, ... Don't use a calculator!

Can you find a formula for the length of the $(n + 1)$th arm in terms of the nth arm?

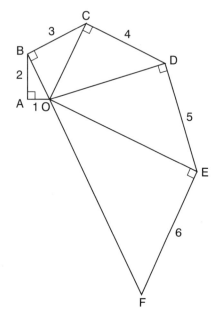

3 Here are some terms of a sequence correct to 4 decimal places. Try to find what the exact values of the terms might be.

1·7321   2·2361   2·6458   3·0000

4 ABC is an equilateral triangle of side 2 units and DEF is a right-angled isosceles triangle whose smaller sides are each 1 unit long.

(a) Explain why $\sin 60° = \dfrac{\sqrt{3}}{2}$.

(b) Use the diagrams to help you write down the exact values of:

    (i) $\cos 60°$

    (ii) $\sin 30°$

    (iii) $\tan 60°$

    (iv) $\tan 45°$

    (v) $\cos 45°$

(c) Use the diagrams to find as many other exact values of trigonometric functions as you can.

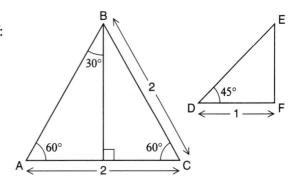

5 Use some of your answers to question **4** to find the exact values of:

(a) $\sin^2 30°$ (*$\sin^2 30°$ is another way to write $(\sin 30°)^2$.*)

(b) $\sin^2 30° + \cos^2 30°$ (c) $\sqrt{2}\cos 45°$ (d) $\cos 45° \times \sin 45°$

Sometimes, even with angles which do not have exact trigonometric values, it may be useful to use the trigonometric expression rather than evaluating it.

6 Here is a regular pentagon ABCDE of side a, inscribed inside a circle with centre at O.

(a) Calculate $\angle EAB$ and $\angle OAB$.

(b) Find an expression for the radius of the circle in terms of trigonometric functions.

(c) Find an expression for the length AX.

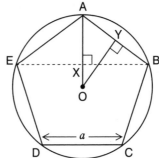

7 Don't use a calculator for any part of this question.

(a) A and X are two vertices of a regular hexagon of side 5 cm. What are the possible values of the distance AX?

(b) B and Y are two vertices of a regular hexagon of side d cm. What are the possible values of the distance BY?

4 Compounding errors

A Measurement

●Thinking point

Several hundred years ago, Galileo thought of a method of finding the speed
of light. It involved two people. Each had a lantern and they stood on two
hills several miles apart. At nightfall the person on the first hill showed their
lamp and started counting in seconds. As soon as the other person saw the
light they showed their lantern. The first person stopped timing as soon as
they saw the second light.

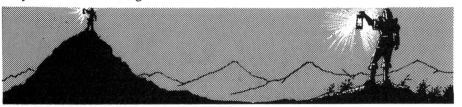

Two people tried this on two hills about 3 miles apart. The time between the
first person showing a light and seeing the one on the other hill was
estimated to be about half a second.

They obtained a figure for the speed of light of 12 miles per second.

The actual figure is about 186 000 miles per second!

Why was their experimental figure so far out?

Measurements can never be exact. There is always some **uncertainty**. This is
sometimes called **experimental error** or just **error**.

We usually assume, unless told otherwise, that there is an uncertainty of $\pm \frac{1}{2}$ unit
in the last digit of any measurement.

So a written result of 12 mm implies that it is 12 ± 0.5 mm or between 11·5 and
12·5 mm.

A written figure of 12·0 mm implies the length is 12.0 ± 0.05 mm. Therefore
12·0 mm implies a greater accuracy than 12 mm.

> **A1** Write down the minimum and maximum possible values for the
> following measured quantities.
>
> (a) 64 °C   (b) 30·4 m/s   (c) 1·50 volts   (d) 2·05 s

> **A2** Amy, Choy and Alan were asked to measure the width of a piece of
> paper with a ruler. They decided to give the mean of their separate
> measurements. The final figure they wrote down was 207·3333 mm.
>
> Was this a sensible experimental result?
> Explain your answer carefully. What would *you* have written down?

40

A3   Graham used a pair of digital scales to find the mass of a single multilink cube. The scale read to the nearest gram, so he wrote his result as 4 ± 0.5 g. He then wrote that the mass of 1000 of these cubes would have a mass of 4 ± 0.5 kg if he used the same set of scales. Was Graham correct? Explain your reasons carefully.

A4   Write down the minimum and maximum possible values for the following quantities.

(a) $23 \pm 1°C$ (b) 112.5 ± 0.25 m   (c) 1.5 ± 0.3 volt

A5   Here is the plan of a rectangular garden. All the measurements are correct to the nearest metre (± 0.5 m).

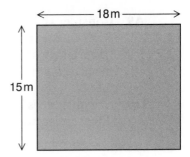

(a) Find:
   (i) the maximum possible perimeter of the garden
   (ii) the minimum possible perimeter of the garden

(b) Claire says 'The perimeter of the garden is 66 ± 2 metres.' Is she correct?

Consider the case of two measurements where $a = w \pm x$ and $b = y \pm z$.
The sum of a and b is $(w \pm x) + (y \pm z) = (w + y) \pm (x + z)$.

> When measurements are given in ± form, the uncertainty of the sum of the measurements is the sum of the individual uncertainties.

A6   Show that the statement in the box above is true for the uncertainty in the length of a rod made from two smaller rods placed end to end, one 2.5 ± 0.01 m and the other 4.2 ± 0.02 m. Make all the steps in your working clear.

A7 The gable end of a house is 100 layers of bricks high.
Each brick is on a layer of mortar.
Each brick is 65 ± 1 mm high and the mortar is 10 ± 2 mm thick.

(a) What is the maximum and minimum possible height of the house?

(b) If there was a whole estate made from these houses, why is it unlikely that any of them would be either of these heights?

A8 When archaeologists work out the age of objects, their figures are never exact. There is always some uncertainty about them.

The ages found by radiocarbon dating of two pieces of Chinese ironware are given as 2380 ± 90 years and 2060 ± 70 years. What, according to these figures, is the greatest and smallest age difference between these two items of ironware?

A9 Consider the two measurements a and b, where $a = w \pm x$ and $b = y \pm z$. Find a similar rule to the one on page 41 which gives the uncertainty arising in the case of the *difference* of these two measurements. Test your rule with some numbers of your own.

A10 The distances between bridges are marked on a canal walk guide. They are accurate to ± 50 m.

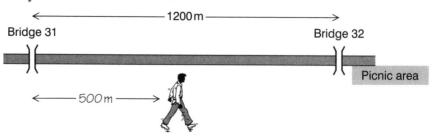

Tariq reckons he has walked 500 metres give or take 20 metres from bridge 31 towards bridge 32. What is the least and greatest distance he may need to walk to reach bridge 32?

Thinking point

Thomas says that an alternative way of writing, for example, 23 metres to the nearest metre is 23 ± 1 m.

Why is he wrong? What should he have written?

The minimum possible value for a quantity is called the **lower bound**, and the maximum possible value is called the **upper bound**.

A11 This sketch shows the dimensions of a plot of land; they are correct to the nearest metre.

Work out the lower bound and the upper bound for the area of the plot of land.

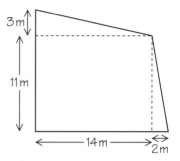

A12 Here is a table from a book about navigating small boats. It gives the uncertainty of compass bearings and the depth found using an echo-sounder.

System	Calm conditions	Moderate conditions	Rough conditions
Compass bearing	± 2°	± 5°	± 10°
Depth by echo-sounder	± 5% of depth	± 5% of depth	± 5% of depth

Three boats are in a race and the weather is moderate.

(a) One of the echo-sounders records a depth of 20 m. Between what two values could the depth be?

(b) Two of the boats, A and B, are 10 km apart. B is due east of A.

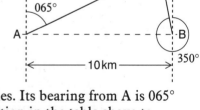

A third boat C is getting into difficulties. Its bearing from A is 065° and from B it is 350°. Use the information in the table above to make a scale drawing showing the region where C might be located.

A13 The coefficient of friction, μ (pronounced 'mew'), is the measure of the friction between a block of material and the surface on which it is moving.

$$\mu = \frac{\text{the force needed to just move the block}}{9 \cdot 8 \times \text{mass of the block}}$$

The force needed to just move a block of stone of mass 50 ± 1 kg is 291 ± 0·5 N. What are the upper and lower bounds for the coefficient of friction?

A14 According to an athletics magazine, a good under-16 female athlete should run 100 metres in 14·5 seconds. Assuming that a 100 m course is correct to the nearest metre and that the timings are correct to the nearest 0·1 second, what are the maximum and minimum possible average speeds of an athlete over this distance for this time? Give your answer in metres per second.

A15 Some students are finding the refractive index of light in a glass block.
This is calculated from the formula

$$n \text{ (the refractive index)} = \frac{\sin i}{\sin r}$$

where i is the angle of incidence and r the angle of refraction.

If $i = 60 \pm 0.5°$ and $r = 43 \pm 0.5°$, find the upper and lower bounds for the refractive index of the glass block.

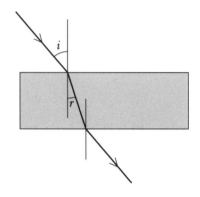

A16 The formula connecting the two sides a and b, the included angle C and the area A of a triangle is $A = \frac{1}{2}ab \sin C$.

Calculate the upper and lower bounds for the area of a triangle when $a = 10 \pm 0.05$ cm, $b = 10 \pm 0.05$ cm and $C = 120 \pm 1°$.

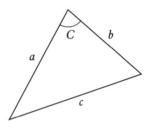

A17 Radar can be used to find the position of rain clouds.
The radar transmitter sends out a signal which is reflected from the cloud.
A radar map on a screen shows how far away the cloud is.

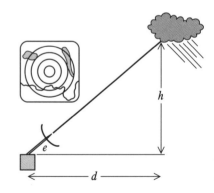

If the radar antenna is tilted slightly, the radar beam will just miss the cloud so no signal will be reflected back.
When this happens, h, the cloud height, is given by the formula $h = d \tan e$.
The distance d is read from the radar screen.

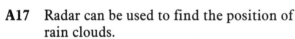

(a) If d is 40 ± 2 km and $e = 5 \pm 0.1°$, find the possible range in the cloud height.

(b) In actual fact, the radar beam gives the direct distance from the antenna to the cloud, not the distance d along the ground.
For $d \approx 40$ km and $e = 5°$, is it reasonable to assume that these two distances are approximately equal?

B   Uncertain about uncertainty

When a measurement is given as 1.5 ± 0.3 volts, for example, we say that the measurement 1.5 volts has an **absolute error** (uncertainty) of ± 0.3 volts. This means we know that the voltage lies between 1.2 volts and 1.8 volts.

 Thinking point

Which do you think seems the more accurate measurement, 1 ± 0.3 volts or 10 ± 0.3 volts? Why?

Sometimes it is more useful to know the **relative error** (uncertainty). This is usually given by the absolute error as a percentage of the measured value. So 25 ± 0.5 mm is a relative error of $(\frac{0.5}{25} \times 100) = 2\%$,

but 50 ± 0.5 mm is a relative error of $(\frac{0.5}{50} \times 100) = 1\%$.

Relative errors are generally only given correct to 1 or 2 significant figures. They are very useful because they allow the uncertainties in different measurements to be compared.

B1 Calculate the upper and lower bounds for the following quantities.

(a) 45 mm $\pm$ 2%   (b) 35 °C $\pm$ 1%   (c) 12 volts $\pm$ 5%

B2 Calculate, to 2 s.f., the relative errors of these quantities.

(a) 2 ± 0.5 mm   (b) 20 ± 0.5 mm

(c) 40 ± 2 m/s   (d) 85 ± 1°C

B3 The side of a square is measured as 100 cm $\pm$ 2%.
Calculate, to 1 s.f., the relative error in the area of the square.

 Thinking point

The length of the side of a square is given as 100 cm $\pm$ 2%.
How could you find the *absolute* error in its area?

B4 Which of these is the more accurate measurement,
      1 km $\pm$ 1 cm or 15 m $\pm$ 0.01%?
Explain your answer.

C Worse and worse

C1 On 11 March 1929, Henry Segrave broke the world land speed record. His car was called Golden Arrow.

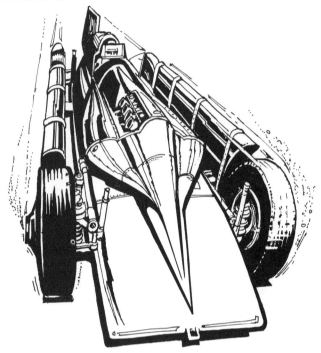

(a) It took him 15·56 seconds to cover the measured mile. A lot of newspapers quoted his speed for this as 231·362 46 miles an hour. A mathematics magazine commented at the time that this figure was incorrect. Explain what was meant by this.

(b) The time of 15·56 seconds implied that it was measured with an uncertainty of ± 0·005 seconds. This figure gives a relative error of about 0·03%. To what accuracy would the measured mile need to be marked to give the same relative error?

(There are 1760 yards in a mile and 36 inches in a yard.)

C2 A speedometer in a car has a relative error (accuracy) of ± 5%. A stopwatch has an accuracy of ± 0·1%.

What are the maximum and minimum distances travelled by the car in one minute timed by this stopwatch, when the speedometer shows 100 km/h?

C3 Choose some numbers of your own to investigate the truth of the statement below. Write a short summary of your findings.

> When two quantities are subtracted, the relative error in the result can be far greater than the relative error in either of the quantities.

C4 The formula $Q = UA(t_1 - t_2)$ gives the heat loss in watts through a window of area A m² when the inside temperature is t_1°C and the outside temperature t_2°C. U is the thermal transmittance which, for ordinary windows, has a value of 5·7 watts/m² °C.

(a) Calculate the heat loss through a 2 m² window when the inside temperature is 16 °C and the outside temperature is 14 °C.

(b) Find the upper and lower bounds for the heat loss if the temperatures are measured to the nearest 1°C.

(c) Look at your answers to (a) and (b). What can you say about the uncertainty in the heat loss when the temperatures are measured to the nearest 1°C?

C5 A steel supply company sells sheets of steel 2500 mm by 1250 mm, with a stated tolerance in dimensions of ± 2%.

Work out the maximum and minimum possible dimensions of one of these steel sheets.

C6 An engineering company cuts out blanks from the steel sheets in **C5**. The blanks are 400 mm by 160 mm with a tolerance of ± 1 mm. They can be cut out in two different ways.

(a) Using method A, what is the maximum possible number of blanks that could be cut from:

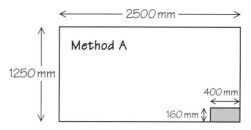

  (i) the length of the sheet
  (ii) the width of the sheet
  (iii) the whole sheet?

(b) What is the minimum number of blanks which can be cut out?

(c) The company decides to try cutting the blanks out in a different arrangement (method B).

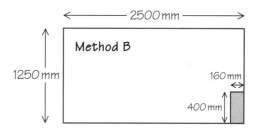

  (i) What is the maximum number of blanks which may be cut in this way?
  (ii) What is the minimum number possible?

(d) Which method, A or B, is the most economical way to cut blanks from the metal sheets? Give a reason for your answer.

C7 Calculate the relative errors for each of these.

(a) The area of a circle of radius 10 ± 0.5 cm, taking π as 3.14.

(b) The volume of a cube of side 10 cm $\pm 1\%$.

(c) The volume of a square-based pyramid of height 20 cms $\pm 5\%$ and base area 100 cm^2 $\pm 5\%$.

(d) The potential drop V (in volts) across a resistor R of 10 ohms $\pm 5\%$, carrying a current I of 5 amps $\pm 5\%$.

(The formula for Ohm's Law is $V = IR$.)

C8 The scale factor for an enlargement is found by dividing a length on the image by the corresponding length on the object.

Find the maximum and minimum possible values for the scale factor when the length on the image is 5 ± 0.1 cm and the corresponding length on the object is 1 ± 0.1 cm.

Hamid is convinced that there is a connection between the relative errors in two quantities and the relative error in their product. To enable him to investigate a range of numbers quickly he decides to use a spreadsheet.

This is part of his spreadsheet, showing the formulas he used.

	A	B	C
1	X	200	23
2	Y	50	674
3	% error in X	1	1
4	% error in Y	3	3
5	Max. X	=B1*(1+B3/100)	=C1*(1+C3/100)
6	Min. X	=B1*(1-B3/100)	=C1*(1-C3/100)
7	Max. Y	=B2*(1+B4/100)	=C2*(1+C4/100)
8	Min. Y	=B2*(1-B4/100)	=C2*(1-C4/100)
9	Max. -ve % uncertainty in XY	=100*(B1*B2-B6*B8)/(B1*B2)	=100*(C1*C2-C6*C8)/(C1*C2)
10	Max. +ve % uncertainty in XY	=100*(B5*B7-B1*B2)/(B1*B2)	=100*(C5*C7-C1*C2)/(C1*C2)
11	Mean % uncertainty in XY	=(B9+B10)/2	=(C9+C10)/2

B5 refers to the maximum value of X calculated by adding (B3)% to B1.

B6 refers to the minimum value of X calculated by subtracting (B3)% from B1.

Similarly for the maximum (B7) and minimum (B8) values of Y.

B9 and B10 refer to the maximum percentage difference above and below the value of XY (B1*B2).

In B11 the mean of these two figures is calculated.

Here are the results for X = 200 ± 1% and Y = 50 ± 3%. These give the mean relative error in the product XY (200 × 50) of 4%.

Also shown are the figures for X = 23 ± 1% and Y = 674 ± 3% (XY = 23 × 674).

	A	B	C
1	X	200	23
2	Y	50	674
3	% error in X	1	1
4	% error in Y	3	3
5	Max. X	202	23.23
6	Min. X	198	22.77
7	Max. Y	51.5	694.22
8	Min. Y	48.5	653.78
9	Max. −ve % uncertainty in XY	3.97	3.97
10	Max. +ve % uncertainty in XY	4.03	4.029999999999
11	Mean % uncertainty in XY	4	3.999999999999

C9 From Hamid's figures, what seems to be the approximate relationship between the relative errors on each number, X and Y, and the relative error in the product XY?

C10 Investigate further the approximate relationship in **C9**. For example, when does it break down?

You could use a spreadsheet like Hamid did or you may prefer to write a program, perhaps using a programmable calculator, or …

Write a short report mentioning anything interesting you find.

C11 Moira says, 'It looks as if the relative error in the product of two quantities is approximately equal to the sum of their individual errors. This might mean that the relative error when two quantities are divided is approximately equal to the difference of their individual errors.'

Investigate to see if Moira's guess is correct.

Options

Investigate the truth of at least one of these statements.

- The widths of two panels are roughly equal. Both their widths have been measured with an uncertainty of x%. Is the relative uncertainty in the width of the two panels placed side by side approximately 2x%?

- Two lengths of a rectangle are both measured with a relative error of x%. So the relative error of the area of the rectangle is x^2%.

- The greatest possible error as a result of calculating with a quantity raised to a power, say n, is the relative error multiplied by n.

D The smaller the better!

D1 Here are the exact answers to some calculations involving squaring the contents of the brackets.

$(1 + 0·1)^2 = 1·21$ $(1 + 0·04)^2 = 1·0816$ $(1 + 0·01)^2 = 1·0201$
$(1 + 0·02)^2 = 1·0404$

(a) Use the calculations to check this approximate rule.

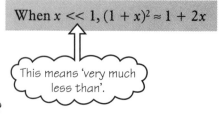

When $x \ll 1, (1 + x)^2 \approx 1 + 2x$

This means 'very much less than'.

(b) Does the rule work for cases like $0·93^2$? Investigate.

(c) Does the approximation improve for smaller values of x?

(d) Find, by trial and improvement, when the difference between the true and approximate values is less than 1%.
In other words, how much smaller than 1 does 'very much less than' actually mean?

We can use the approximation above to help in problems involving relative errors, but first we need a little algebra:

$a\%$ is equivalent to $\dfrac{a}{100}$ which is $0·01a$.

So $a\%$ of a quantity x is $x \times 0·01a$.

We know that if a quantity x has a relative uncertainty of $a\%$, its value must lie between $x - (a\% \text{ of } x)$ and $x + (a\% \text{ of } x)$.

This is the same as being between $x(1 - 0·01a)$ and $x(1 + 0·01a)$.

This means that x^2 must be between $x^2(1 - 0·01a)^2$ and $x^2(1 + 0·01a)^2$.

If we can assume that $0·01a$ is small compared with 1, then we can use the approximation in **D1**.

So the value of x^2 lies between $x^2(1 - 0·02a)$ and $x^2(1 + 0·02a)$.

If you look at the statement six lines above, you should see that this is the same as saying that the relative error in x^2 is $2a\%$.

If the relative uncertainty of a quantity is $a\%$, the relative uncertainty of its square is $2a\%$.

D2 The rule above can be very useful, but it is only an approximation. Investigate how good an approximation it is for various values of the relative uncertainty ($a\%$).

The spreadsheet or computer program you used for **C10** might be adapted to help here.

E   Super accuracy

It is now possible to measure the distance to the moon with an uncertainty of ± 5 cm! The moon is about $380\,000$ km away.

With this sort of accuracy, the percentage relative uncertainty would be too small to compare quantities easily. Instead, relative errors are given in **parts per million** (ppm) rather than parts per 100 (%).

E1   What is an uncertainty of $0\cdot01\%$ as a ppm uncertainty?

E2   Give the ± 5 cm uncertainty in the distance to the moon in ppm.

E3   The speed of light is probably one of the most accurately known quantities. In the 1960s it was found to be $299\,792\cdot56 \pm 0\cdot11$ km/s. What is this uncertainty in ppm?

E4   From your answer to **E2** you may think that even ppm is too large. What do you think should be used after ppm?

Summary

- When dealing with measured quantities, it is safe to assume that there is an uncertainty of $\pm 0\cdot5$ in the last digit, unless told otherwise.

  So a figure of $12\cdot4\,°C$ implies that the actual temperature is in the range $12\cdot35\,°C$ to $12\cdot45\,°C$. We say that it has a **lower bound** of $12\cdot35\,°C$ and an **upper bound** of $12\cdot45\,°C$.

- A quantity quoted as $65\cdot6 \pm 0\cdot2$ cm has an **absolute error** (uncertainty) of $0\cdot2$ cm.

- The **relative error** is the absolute error as a percentage of the measured value, so $65\cdot6 \pm 0\cdot2$ is a relative error of about $0\cdot3\%$.

- When quantities are added or subtracted, the combined error is the sum of the individual errors.

- When quantities are added, the relative error of the result lies between the individual relative errors.

- When quantities are subtracted, very large relative errors can result if the two quantities are close together in size.

- The relative error when several quantities are multiplied or divided is approximately equal to the sum of the relative errors of the quantities.

- Very small relative errors are given in **parts per million** (ppm).

5 Using graphs to solve equations

A Times past

Solving an equation like $6x - 12 = 0$ should not present a problem!

In fact, neither should any equation of the form $ax + b = 0$, where a and b represent numbers. (In the example above, $a = 6$ and $b = {}^-12$.)

You probably solved the equation just by looking at it (this method is called **inspection**), or by doing it on paper or in your head:

$$6x - 12 = 0$$
$$6x = 12$$
$$x = 2$$

This particular method was not used much until the Arab mathematician al-Khwarizmi showed it in a maths text in about the year AD 820.

In fact, the word algebra may have come from the Arabic word 'al-jabr' which means 'restoring' (adding terms to each side of an equation to remove negative quantities).

A method which was widely used in Ancient Egypt, India and China until a few hundred years ago, was called the **method of false position**. Arab mathematicians brought it to Europe in the Middle Ages.

This is how the method works (using modern notation).

The equation to be solved is $ax + b = 0$.   (*a, b* are numbers and *x* is the unknown.)

Guess two solutions. Call these g_1 and g_2.
(We use the subscripts $_1$ and $_2$ to make the algebra easier to read.)

Then $ag_1 + b = f_1$ (*f* stands for false value.)
          $ag_2 + b = f_2$

The solution to the equation is given by the formula $x = \dfrac{f_1 g_2 - f_2 g_1}{f_1 - f_2}$

This may seem a very complicated way to solve such a simple equation, but it is a method which works for all equations of the type $ax + b = 0$.

It was a simple formula to learn as the arrangement of letters in the formula is symmetrical.

Another reason for the popularity of the method of false position was that the algebraic expressions in those times were not as easy to read or understand as those we use today. Symbols for unknown quantities, for example x and y, were not used until the 17th century.

Different mathematicians used different symbols for, say, x and x^2.

- Pacioli (1494): Trouame.1.nº.che giotō al suo q̄dratº facia .12.

  Modern form: $x + x^2 = 12$.

- Vander Hoecke (1514): 4 Se. – 51 Pri. – 30 N. dit is ghelijc $45\frac{3}{5}$.

  Modern form: $4x^2 - 51x - 30 = 45\frac{3}{5}$.

- Ghaligai (1521): 1□ e 32 cº – 320 numeri.

  Modern form: $x^2 + 32x = 320$.

- Rudolff (1525): Sit 1 δ aequatus 12 χ – 36.

  Modern form: $x^2 = 12x - 36$.

- Cardan (1545): cub⁹ p: 6 reb⁹ aeqlis 20.

  Modern form: $x^3 + 6x = 20$.

A1 Use the method of false position to solve these equations.

(a) $4x + 8 = 0$ (b) $^-2x - 10 = 0$ (c) $^-4x + 12 = 0$

Check your answers using your normal method.

A2 Prove the formula for x which is given by the method of false position for the general equation $ax + b = 0$.

A3 (a) Write down a modern formula to solve equations of the form
$$ax + b = c,$$
where a, b and c are numbers and x is the unknown.

(b) Use your formula to solve these, giving your answers correct to one decimal place.

(i) $6 \cdot 5x + 1 \cdot 7 = 123 \cdot 5$ (ii) $1 \cdot 97x - 3 \cdot 76 = 21 \cdot 74$

(iii) $^-3 \cdot 1x + 7 \cdot 21 = 67 \cdot 21$ (iv) $^-8 \cdot 1x - 6 \cdot 7 = ^-56 \cdot 21$

(c) Check your answers to (b) by substituting each solution back into the original equation.

An equation which only includes powers of x (for example x^2, x^{10}) and numbers (for example 2, $\frac{2}{15}$) is called a **polynomial equation**.

So far all the equations in this chapter have been **linear** – they have only involved x's.

We classify polynomial equations by the highest power of x in them, where x is the unknown.

Those whose highest power of x is x^2 are called **quadratic** equations. These are all quadratic equations:

$$4x^2 + 4x - 18 = 0, \ x^2 = 74, \ 2a^2 - a = 15$$

If the highest power of x is x^3, they are called **cubic** equations. For example, $x^3 - 2x = 16$, $4x^3 + 2x^2 - x + 16 = 0$ and $x^3 = 19$.

These are **quartic** equations: $x^4 - 2x^3 = 16$, $4x^4 + 2x^3 - x^2 + 16 = 0$ and $b^4 = 19$.

A4 In *Book Y4* you solved equations by factorisation.
This is sometimes called finding the roots of the equation.

$$x^2 + 2x - 15 = 0$$
$$(x + 5)(x - 3) = 0$$
So either $x + 5 = 0$ or $x - 3 = 0$
So either $x = {}^-5$ or $x = 3$
The solutions are ${}^-5$ and 3.

Factorise and solve each of these quadratic equations.

(a) $x^2 + 7x + 10 = 0$ (b) $x^2 + x - 20 = 0$ (c) $x^2 - 4x - 21 = 0$

It is thought that Indian mathematicians may have discovered this formula to solve quadratic equations about 2500 years ago:

For the quadratic $x^2 + bx + c = 0$, $x = {}^-\frac{1}{2}b + \sqrt{(\frac{1}{4}b^2 - c)}$

A5 Use the formula to solve the equations in **A4**.
Compare your answers with those you found by factorising.
What do you notice?

─── *Thinking point* ───

How can the formula be made to give the second root?
(**Hint:** $4 = {}^-2 \times {}^-2$ as well as 2×2!)

A6 Use the formula to solve these quadratic equations.

(a) $x^2 + 4x - 10 = 0$ (b) $x^2 - 2x - 3 = 0$ (c) $x^2 - x - 10 = 0$

B When algebra fails!

There is a formula for solving cubic equations, but the algebra is very complex. However, some may be factorised, like this one.

$$x^3 - 7x - 6 = 0$$
$$(x + 1)(x^2 - x - 6) = 0 \quad (x = {}^-1 \text{ is an obvious solution})$$
$$(x + 1)(x - 3)(x + 2) = 0 \quad (\text{factorising the second bracket})$$

So either $(x + 1) = 0$ or $(x - 3) = 0$ or $(x + 2) = 0$.

Therefore $x = {}^-1$ or $x = 3$ or $x = {}^-2$.

The solutions are $x = {}^-1, 3$ and ${}^-2$.

 Challenge

Can you solve this cubic equation by factorisation?
$$x^3 + 2x^2 - 19x - 20 = 0$$

In 14th and 15th century Europe, large national competitions were held to see who could solve certain cubic or quartic equations!

Many equations, especially those in engineering, cannot be solved just by using algebraic manipulation, factorisation or formulas. In other words, it is not possible, however many algebraic tricks are tried, to end up with $x = \ldots$

In cases like this, trial and improvement can be used. This is sometimes called the **numerical solution** of equations. Chinese mathematicians used this method in the 13th and 14th centuries and were probably the first to solve equations like ${}^-x^4 + 763\,200x^2 - 40\,642\,560\,000 = 0$ by trial and improvement!

Another method is to use graphs. This is made easier if you have a graphical calculator or a graph/function-plotting program.

In this example, the graph of $y = x^2 - x - 6$ is plotted to solve the equation:

$$x^2 - x - 6 = 0$$

There are two solutions:

$$x = 3 \text{ and } x = {}^-2$$

These are also solutions to the equations:

$$x^2 - x = 6$$
$$x^2 = x + 6$$

and $x^2 - 6 = x$

Can you explain why?

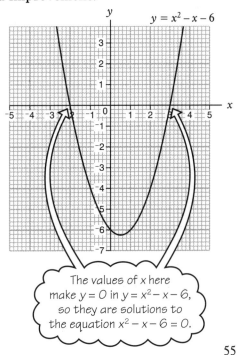

The values of x here make $y = 0$ in $y = x^2 - x - 6$, so they are solutions to the equation $x^2 - x - 6 = 0$.

B1–B5 You need worksheet YX1–6.

B6–B8 You need worksheet YX1–7.

55

B9 Draw the graph of $y = x^2 - 5x + 3$ for values of x from $^-2$ to 8.
Use the graph to solve these equations.
(You shouldn't need to draw another curve, only straight lines.)

(a) $x^2 - 5x + 3 = 0$ (b) $x^2 - 5x + 3 = 5$

(c) $x^2 - 5x + 3 = 2x$ (d) $x^2 - 7x + 3 = 0$

Check your answers by using a graph-plotting device.

Rearranging the terms of an equation can suggest different graphs which could be plotted to solve the original equation.

For example, $x^3 + 3x^2 - 2x - 6 = 0$ can be solved graphically in several ways.

- By drawing $y = x^3 + 3x^2 - 2x - 6$ and finding where it cuts the x-axis.
- By drawing $y = x^3$ and $y = {}^-3x^2 + 2x + 6$ and finding the x-coordinate of the point or points where two curves cross.
- The original equation could even be rearranged to give $x(x^2 + 3x - 2) = 6$ and then finding where the two curves $y = x^2 + 3x - 2$ and $y = \dfrac{6}{x}$ cut.

B10 Write down at least three sets of different graphs which could be used to solve the equation $x^3 + x^2 - 15x = 10$.

Draw each of your pairs of graphs and check that each gives the same solution. You may find a graph-plotting device useful!

You can obtain very accurate solutions to an equation by using a graph-plotting device.

Here is how you could use a graph-plotter to solve the equation $\dfrac{x^3}{3} - x^2 = 2x + 1$.

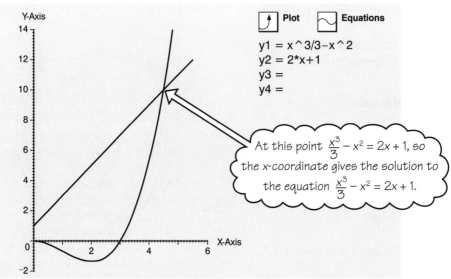

56

Zooming in on the crossing point (or altering the axis scales) can give the roots or solutions as precisely as you want. Some graphical calculators have a 'trace' facility which may also be useful. Here are enlargements of the graph on page 56.

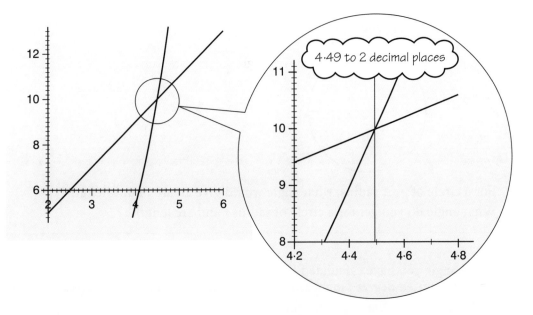

B11 Use whichever device you have to find both roots of the equation $2x^2 + 3x - 10 = 0$ by zooming in. Find each root correct to 2 decimal places. Check your answers.

B12 The equation $x^3 + 2x^2 + 10x = 20$ was first solved by the mathematician Fibonacci in the 13th century. He was accused of copying the answer from a Chinese mathematician he met on a journey to China!

Solve the equation graphically, giving your answer correct to 1 decimal place.

⬤ *Thinking point*

How could you solve equations like $5\sin x = 3$ or $100\sin x = 50 - x$?

(Do not solve these equations now, but explain how you *could* solve them using a graph plotter.)

Thinking point

For an arc subtended by an angle ϕ at the centre of the circle:

$$\text{arc length } (l) = \frac{\phi}{360°} \times \text{circumference}$$

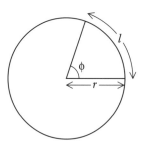

For a circle of unit radius, what angle would give an arc of unit length?

What angle do you get for a circle of radius r and arc length r?

The angle you have calculated is called a **radian**.

You have used degrees to measure angles, but you can also use radians.

There are 2π radians in a full turn.

So $1°$ is equivalent to $\frac{2\pi}{360}$ radians, which is approximately 0.017 radians.

One radian is about $57°$.

The symbol for radians is ^{c}, but if no symbol is given (^{c} or $°$) then, by convention, the angle is in radians.

Your calculator can probably work in radians or degrees. Find out how to change from one to another on your own model.

B13 (a) Convert these angles from degrees to radians. Express your answer as a multiple of π, and then as a decimal to 3 decimal places.

   (i) $90°$ (ii) $270°$ (iii) $60°$
   (iv) $45°$ (v) $70°$ (vi) $151°$

(b) Convert these angles from radians into degrees (to 1 decimal place).

   (i) $\frac{\pi}{6}$ (ii) $\frac{3\pi}{4}$ (iii) $\frac{2\pi}{3}$ (iv) 5 (v) 2 (vi) 1.66

B14 Find the value of the following trigonometric functions.

   (a) $\sin\frac{\pi}{6}$ (b) $\cos\frac{\pi}{6}$ (c) $\tan\frac{\pi}{4}$

   (d) $\sin\frac{\pi}{2}$ (e) $\tan 1$ (f) $\sin 0.05$

B15 Find the following angles in radians. If you can, express them as multiples of π. (cos⁻¹ means 'the angle whose cosine is'.)

(a) $\cos^{-1} 0{\cdot}5$ (b) $\sin^{-1} 1$ (c) $\tan^{-1} 0{\cdot}5$ (d) $\cos^{-1} 0{\cdot}3$

Equations involving both trigonometric functions and polynomials in x, for example $\sin x = x$, $\cos 2x = x^2 + 5x$ and $\cos x + \sin \dfrac{x}{2} = \dfrac{x}{2}$, are almost always solved for x measured in radians.

B16 You need worksheet YX1–8.

You have seen that very accurate solutions to polynomial equations can be found using graph-plotting devices. The same is true for this type of equation. Here is how you would solve the equation $5 \sin x = \dfrac{3x}{2}$.

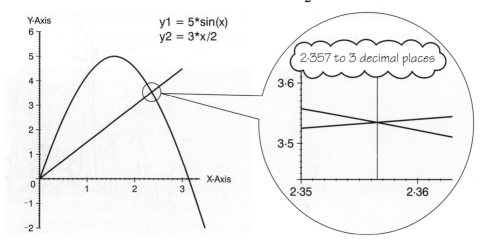

B17 Solve the equation $100 \cos \dfrac{x}{2} - x = 0$ to 2 decimal places.

B18 Solve $\cos x = x^2$ to 2 decimal places.

Thinking point

Show that if you solved the equation in **B17** in degrees you would obtain a different value for x.

Options

- 'The sine and cosine of small angles are approximately equal to their size.' Investigate.

- One advantage of working with radians is that the area of a sector radius r, angle ϕ^c, is $\frac{1}{2}r^2\phi$. Show why this is true.

Mixed bag 1

1 The length of a rectangle is increased by 30% and its width decreased by 20%. What effect does this have on its area?

2 Find the values of these letters. Each one stands for a different digit.

$$\begin{array}{r} TWO \\ \times\ TWO \\ \hline THREE \end{array}$$

3 The Babylonian system of fractions used 60 and 60^2 as denominators. They did not usually bother to write these down. So 7, 30 would mean $\frac{7}{60} + \frac{30}{3600} = \frac{450}{3600}$, which is equivalent to $\frac{1}{8}$.

Write these fractions as Babylonian fractions.

(a) $\frac{1}{4}$ (b) $\frac{1}{2}$ (c) $\frac{1}{9}$ (d) $\frac{1}{90}$

4 This rectangle is inscribed inside a circle of radius 10 cm.

Show that the area of the rectangle is $400 \sin \phi \times \cos \phi$.

Use this result to show that for the rectangle to have the maximum area it must be a square.

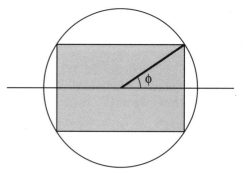

5 x is the value of the nth term in the sequence 49, 56, 63, ..., x. Express n in terms of x.

6 What is the last digit in $3^{123} - 2^{123}$?

7 Find the height of a pyramid or cone when its volume is numerically the same as the area of its base. (Assume you are working in cm, cm² and cm³.)

8 Find the area of the triangle formed by the x-axis, the line $y = x$ and the line $x + 3y = 12$.

9 What fraction of this square is the shaded region?

10 On a clockface the hours 2, 4, 7 and 11 are joined up to form a quadrilateral. Find each of its interior angles.

6 Congruency

A Some recapping

Two triangles are said to be **congruent** if they are equal in all respects, that is,
three angles and three sides in one triangle are equal to the *corresponding* three
angles and three sides in the other triangle. The word 'congruent' comes from a
Latin word meaning 'agree' or 'fall together'.
Two triangles are congruent if any of these conditions are satisfied:

- Two sides of one triangle are equal to
  two sides of the other and the angle
  between these sides (the included angle)
  is equal (**SAS**).

- The three sides of one triangle are
  equal to the three sides of the other
  triangle (**SSS**).

- Two angles and a side of one triangle are
  equal to the angles and the corresponding
  side of the other (**ASA**).

- Each triangle is right-angled and
  the hypotenuse and one side of one
  triangle is equal to the hypotenuse and
  a side of the other triangle (**RHS**).

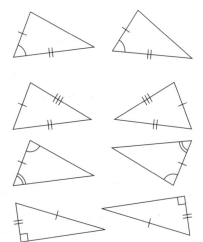

A1 Shown below are three triangles, ABC, DEF and GHI.
They are not drawn to scale. All lengths are given in cm.

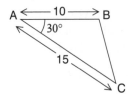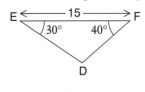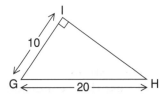

Which (if any) of these triangles are congruent to any of the ones
below? In each case give the reason (SAS, RHS, ...).
Make a note of which sides and angles correspond.

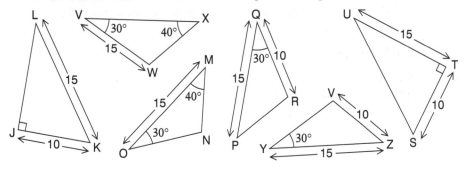

So far we have not proved that the conditions for congruency are true.
In *Book YR+* it was shown that they worked for some cases, but this does not *prove* them.

Here is a proof for one condition (SAS) for congruency.
Read through it carefully.

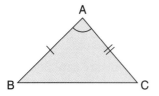 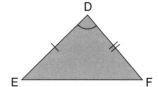

Given ABC and DEF are two triangles where AB = DE, AC = DF and ∠BAC = ∠EDF (the included angles).

To prove The triangles ABC and DEF are congruent.

Proof Place triangle ABC onto triangle DEF so that:
  (i) the point A falls on D,
  (ii) AB lies along DE.

This symbol means therefore.

AB = DE (this was given),
∴ **the point B falls on E.**

AB lies along DE and ∠BAC = ∠EDF,
∴ **AC must lie along DF.**

AC = DF (this was given),
∴ **the point C falls on F.**

Only one straight line can join two points,
∴ **BC coincides with EF.**

∴ All the sides of triangle ABC coincide with the corresponding sides of triangle DEF.
∴ **△ABC is congruent to △DEF.**

There are similar proofs for the other conditions for congruency.
We use these conditions in other proofs.

A2 It is important to realise that whilst some things seem obvious, this does not make them true!
For example, SSS is true for triangles, but is the similar condition SSSS true for quadrilaterals? Give your reasons carefully.

Thinking point

• Two rectangles have the same area and the same perimeter.
Does this mean that they *must* be congruent?

B Using congruent triangles

Congruent triangles can be very useful in proving other results.
It is important to be able to identify the corresponding angles and sides of
congruent triangles, and to know the conditions for congruency.

Read these proofs through carefully.

*To prove that if two sides of a triangle are equal, then the angles opposite
to these sides are equal.*

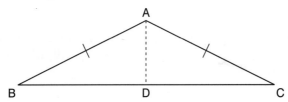

In the triangle ABC, AB = AC.
We have to prove ∠ABC = ∠ACB.

First we need to construct a line, AD, from A which bisects ∠BAC.

In triangles ABD and ACD:

   AB = AC (this is given)
   AD is common to both triangles
   ∠BAD = ∠CAD (because of the construction)
   ∴ Triangles ABD and ACD are congruent (SAS).
So ∠ABC = ∠ACB.

To prove that the diagonals of a parallelogram bisect each other.

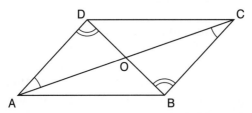

ABCD is a parallelogram whose diagonals AC and DB intersect at O.

In the triangles AOD and COB:

   ∠OAD = ∠OCB (alternate angles)
   ∠ODA = ∠OBC (alternate angles)
   AD = BC (ABCD is a parallelogram)
   ∴ Triangles AOD and COB are congruent (ASA).
So AO = OC and BO = OD.

B1 Prove that the diagonals of a rectangle are equal in length.

B2 Use congruent triangles to prove that the diagonals of a rhombus bisect each other at right-angles.

For most of these questions you will need to sketch a diagram. Always check that your diagram 'fits' the information given – you might need to try again.

B3 Two straight lines AB and CD bisect each other at their point of intersection O. What reasons could you give to convince someone that CB = AD?

B4 The straight lines AB and CD bisect each other at right-angles at O. How would you prove that the straight lines AC, CB, BD and DA are all equal in length?

B5 The mid-points of the sides of an equilateral triangle are joined. How could you convince someone that the resulting triangle is also equilateral?

B6 Triangle PQR is isosceles, with ∠PRQ = ∠PQR. QP and RP are extended (**produced**) to X and Y respectively, so that XQ = YR. Prove that XR and YQ are equal in length.

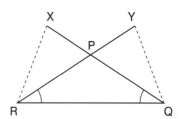

B7 OA and OB are two equal length, straight lines and OC bisects the angle between them. X is any point on OC. Prove that XA = XB.

B8 The mid-points of the sides of a square are joined up to form a quadrilateral. Prove that this quadrilateral is also a square.

B9 The triangles ABC and ABD are congruent to each other. They are acute-angled triangles and are on opposite sides of their common (shared) side AB. A straight line is drawn from C to D cutting AB at O. Prove that OC and OD are equal in length.

B10 The triangle ABC is isosceles; the two equal angles are ∠ACB and ∠ABC. A straight line is drawn from the corner (vertex) A to the mid-point of the side BC. Prove that this line bisects ∠BAC and is perpendicular to BC.

B11 In a triangle ABC, equilateral triangles ABD and ACE are constructed on the sides AB and AC. Prove that BE = CD.

You may find it helpful to work through B12 to B14 with a partner.

B12   The Ancient Greeks were interested in
geometrical constructions which require
only compasses and a straight edge.
For example, they used this method to
bisect angle AOB.

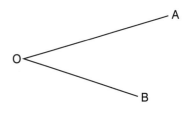

From OA and OB use compasses to
cut off OX and OY equal to each other.

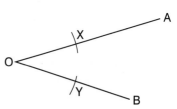

With X as centre and with any
convenient radius, draw an arc.

With Y as centre and with the same
compass radius, draw another arc to cut
the previous one at P.

Join up the points O and P.

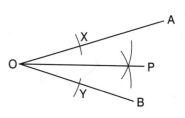

Use congruent triangles to prove that
OP bisects angle AOB.

B13   Here is a method for bisecting a straight line AB.
With centres A and B in turn, and a radius greater than half AB,
draw arcs of circles intersecting at P and Q.

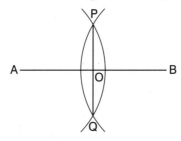

Join P and Q, cutting AB at O.
Prove that O bisects the line AB.

B14   Can you remember how to construct a
regular hexagon using just compasses
and ruler?

Prove that the hexagon is a *regular*
hexagon.

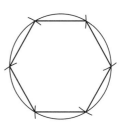

c Odds and ends

You may find it useful to work with a partner on these.

C1 Investigate the truth (or otherwise) of these statements:

(a) If one side of an *equilateral* triangle is equal to one side of another equilateral triangle, then the two triangles are congruent.

(b) In a *right-angled* triangle, if a side and an angle (not the right-angle) are equal to the corresponding side and angle of another right-angled triangle, then the two triangles are congruent.

(c) If one side and one angle of an *isosceles* triangle are equal to the corresponding side and angle of another isosceles triangle, then the two triangles are congruent.

C2 This method can be used to find the width of a river at a point where the banks are fairly straight, without measuring the river width directly.

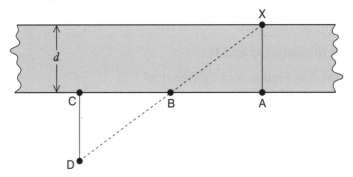

- Start at point A.
- Line up on an object directly across the river (X).
- Take ten paces to a point B.
- Put a stick in the ground.
- Take a further ten paces to C.
- Walk at right-angles to the river-bank to D, where D, B and X all line up.

The distance CD is the width of the river *d*.

Explain why the method works. Why not try it out?

C3 There is more to congruency than congruent triangles!
Investigate or explain these.

(a) If one side of a square is equal in length to one side of another square, then the two squares are congruent.

(b) If the diagonals of a rhombus are equal to the diagonals of another rhombus, then the two rhombuses are congruent.

(c) If one side and the angle formed by the side and the diagonal of a rectangle are equal to the corresponding side and angle of another rectangle, then the two rectangles are congruent.

Option

Investigate conditions for congruency for quadrilaterals (or even pentagons or hexagons). (**Hint**: Don't forget diagonals!)

Summary

- **Congruent** triangles (or any congruent shapes) are identical in shape and size. Pairs of corresponding sides and angles are equal.

- There are several conditions for pairs of triangles to be congruent:

    SAS (two sides and the angle between them equal)
    SSS (all sides equal)
    ASA (two angles and the side between them equal)
    RHS (two right-angled triangles, with the hypotenuse and one other side equal)

For example, $\triangle ABC$ and $\triangle DEF$ are congruent (SAS).

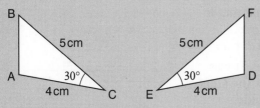

BC, EF and AC, ED are corresponding sides and $\angle BCA$, $\angle FED$ the corresponding angles.

So   AB = FD,
     $\angle ABC = \angle EFD$
and $\angle BAC = \angle EDF$.

7 Good fit?

A In line

In an experiment, the deflection (or sag) of a wooden ruler was measured for
different loads on the ruler. The deflection d was measured in mm and the load w
(which included the weight carrier) in kg.

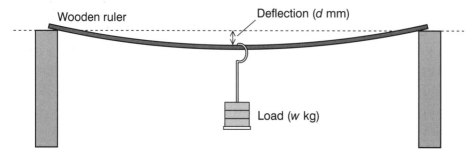

Wooden ruler   Deflection (d mm)

Load (w kg)

These were the results.

w (kg)	2·0	2·5	3·0	3·5	4·0	4·5
d (mm)	5	7	7	8	11	12

Sometimes in an experiment you get an extra piece of data! For this experiment,
common sense tells you that a zero load will give a zero deflection.

If you plot the values of (w, d) and $(0, 0)$, you
can see that the points do not lie on a straight
line. However, you can draw a straight line
like this which nearly fits the data.
This is called the **line of best fit**.

Since the points (w, d) are close to this line, it
looks as if d is roughly proportional to w.
This is sometimes written in short as $d \propto w$.

The symbol $\propto$ means 'proportional to'. It was
first used in the 18th century and was the sign
for Taurus the bull ($\propto$) turned on its side.

The gradient of this straight line is 2·6.

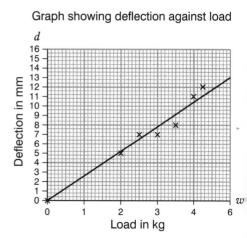

Graph showing deflection against load

Deflection in mm

Load in kg

> **A1** Write down an equation showing the connection between d and w.

The gradient of the line is 2·6, but it is important when dealing with real
quantities to give the units of the gradient. These are $\dfrac{\text{mm}}{\text{kg}}$ so that, strictly
speaking, the gradient is 2·6 mm/kg (for each kilogram of load the deflection
is 2·6 mm).

Experimental results are usually uncertain. This is because measurement can never be exact.

The accuracy of a measurement depends on the instrument used.

In the previous experiment, deflections were measured to the nearest mm. This meant that a certain amount of uncertainty could have been expected in these figures. In fact it would have been suspicious if the results had given a perfectly straight line!

It is doubtful whether two people would agree exactly as to what was the line of best fit. Drawing lines of best fit can be very subjective.

Options

Draw some points on a graph that will give a straight line when fitted by eye. Make copies of the graph. Ask some people to draw a line of best fit.

Compare the gradients and intercepts of their fitted lines.
What conclusions can you make?

When fitting by eye, we draw a straight line which passes as close as possible to all the points. What we need is a mathematical method for doing this.

One way is to compare the experimental values of the deflection with those calculated from the formula, using the fitted-by-eye line. We call these the **observed** and **expected** (from the formula) values. For a good fit, the sum of all the differences (**deviations**) must be as small as possible. We need to adjust the value of the gradient to make this sum as small as possible.

A spreadsheet can help with this task, as could a BASIC or LOGO program.

	A	B	C	D	E
1	Trial gradient =	Load (w kg)	Observed d (mm)	Expected d (mm)	Deviation
2	2.60	2.00	5.00	=$A$2*B2	=C2-D2
3		2.50	7.00	=$A$2*B3	=C3-D3
4	-	3.00	7.00	=$A$2*B4	=C4-D4
5		3.50	8.00	=$A$2*B5	=C5-D5
6		4.00	11.00	=$A$2*B6	=C6-D6
7		4.50	12.00	=$A$2*B7	=C7-D7
8			Sum of the	deviations =	=Sum(E2,E7)

	A	B	C	D	E
1	Trial gradient =	Load (w kg)	Observed d (mm)	Expected d (mm)	Deviation
2	2.60	2.00	5.00	5.20	-0.20
3		2.50	7.00	6.50	0.50
4		3.00	7.00	7.80	-0.80
5		3.50	8.00	9.10	-1.10
6		4.00	11.00	10.40	0.60
7		4.50	12.00	11.70	0.30
8			Sum of the	deviations =	-0.70

A2 (a) Investigate what happens to the sum of the deviations for trial gradients of (i) 2·5 and (ii) 2·7. What do you notice?

(b) Would it be sensible to try a trial value for the gradient of 2·564? Give your reasons.

A3 All the galaxies in the universe are moving apart from each other. The farther away they are, the greater the speed of separation.

The table shows the distances from the Earth and the speeds of recession (separation) from Earth of some very distant galaxies. A billion (10^9) light-years is a distance of $9·5 \times 10^{21}$ km!

Distance (in billions of light-years)	Speed of recession (in thousands of kilometres per second)
0·7	14·9
1·0	21·4
1·6	40·0
1·8	39·0
2·3	48·8
3·1	55·8
3·3	61·4

(a) Plot this data and draw a line of best fit for it. (Make the galaxy distance the x-axis.)

(b) Find the gradient of your line of best fit. The units should be thousands of km/s per billion light-years.

(c) The gradient you have just found is called the Hubble constant. It is named after Edwin Hubble, who in the 1920s found that there was a linear relationship between the distance apart (x) and speed of recession (v) of galaxies. Write down Hubble's law connecting x, v and H, the Hubble constant.

(d) If, in the beginning, all the universe was at one point, Hubble's law can be used to estimate the age of the universe. For example, the galaxy Hydra is now 2·8 billion light-years from Earth and it is moving away from us with a speed of 60 000 km/s. The age of the universe is the number of years Hydra took to cover the 2·8 billion light-years. But first you need to convert times to years, distances to kilometres and speeds to km/year.

How old is the universe? Use some of the data in the table to find a mean value.

B Using the ∝ symbol

If $y \propto x$, then $y = kx$, where k is the multiplier connecting x and y.
For any given set of data, k is called the **constant of proportionality** because
the value of k (the gradient of the line $y = kx$) does not depend on x or y.

B1 In which of these sets of figures is $y \propto x$?
If $y \propto x$, find the value of the constant k in $y = kx$.

(a)
x	2	4	8	10
y	0·8	1·6	3·2	4

(b)
x	30	50	90	110
y	80	160	320	400

(c)
x	20	40	80	100
y	4	200	16	500

(d)
x	2	4	8	10
y	0·5	1·0	2·0	2·5

If $y \propto x$, then we can say that y is **directly proportional** to x.

Other types of proportionality also occur.

Inverse: If y is proportional to the reciprocal of x, we write $y \propto \dfrac{1}{x}$ or $y = k \times \dfrac{1}{x} = \dfrac{k}{x}$.

Square: If $y \propto x^2$ then $y = kx^2$.

Inverse square: If $y \propto \dfrac{1}{x^2}$ then $y = k \times \dfrac{1}{x^2} = \dfrac{k}{x^2}$.

B2 Write down two situations from everyday life where two quantities are
directly proportional to each other and another two where they are
inversely proportional.

B3 Find which of the above types of proportionality these fit, if any.
Where possible, calculate the constant of proportionality, k.

(a)
x	1	2	3	4
y	2	8	18	32

(b)
x	1	2	3	4
y	2	4	6	8

(c)
x	1	2	3	4
y	12	6	4	3

(d)
x	2	8	18	32
y	2	3	4	5

(e)
x	1	2	3	4
y	1	4	9	16

(f)
x	1	2	3	4
y	72	18	8	4·5

B4 Write each of the following statements as an algebraic expression
involving '∝', saying what the symbols you use represent.

(a) The deeper you go into the Earth the hotter it becomes. That is,
the increase in temperature is directly proportional to the depth.

(b) The volume of a sphere is proportional to the cube of its radius.

(c) The gravitational force between two masses is inversely
proportional to the square of their distance apart.

73

C Fit for what?

It can be very useful to have a formula showing the connection between two or more quantities. It sums up the relationship briefly and allows us to make and use predictions.

For example, the formula $h = ai^2$ gives the heat h generated in a second when a current i passes through a component and a is a constant which depends on the units used.

An electrical engineer can use this formula to ensure that no components on a circuit board take too much current and so overheat.

Formulas like these are usually based on a law or theory from physics or chemistry.

Other formulas or relationships may be found just by looking at experimental results and finding the one which fits best. These do not usually have a law or theory in the background. They are called **empirical** relationships.

> **Fitting equations**
>
> If two variables p and q are connected by an equation of the form, say,
>
> $q = a \left(\dfrac{1}{\sqrt{p}} \right) + b$, where a and b are constants, we can find a and b by
>
> plotting q against $\dfrac{1}{\sqrt{p}}$, and drawing a line of best fit. The gradient of
>
> this line gives a and the intercept gives b.
>
> This is called **transforming** the data.
>
> You can see how good the fit is by using a spreadsheet or a graph-drawing program to compare the fitted equation with the original points.

The sales of video cassette recorders (VCRs) can be fitted to a formula.

The number owned over approximately the last fifteen years has been found to be roughly inversely proportional to their price.

These figures may be fitted to the formula, $p = \dfrac{a}{c} + b$ where p is the percentage of households with a VCR and c is the cost in £s of a VCR.

●*Thinking point*

Is it reasonable to assume that the number of VCRs owned depends only on their price? Could any other variables be involved?

A line of best fit can be drawn of p against $\frac{1}{c}$ and the gradient and intercept found.

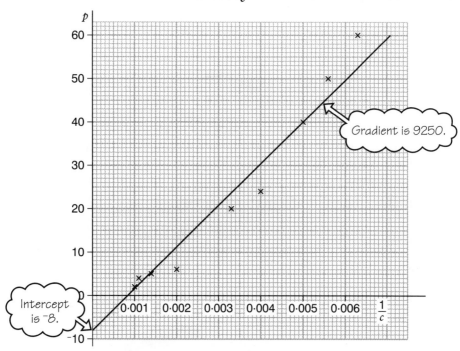

Gradient is 9250.

Intercept is -8.

These give the values of a and b in the equation.

Here is the resulting fitted empirical curve.

As you can see, the match between the 'real' figures and the fitted curve is quite good.

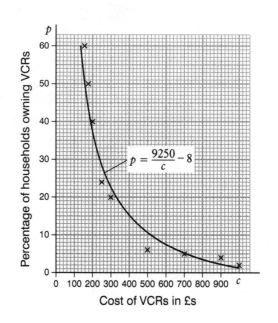

$$p = \frac{9250}{c} - 8$$

Percentage of households owning VCRs

Cost of VCRs in £s

Thinking point

Would you expect the empirical rule to hold when VCRs cost less than £100?

For some of these questions you could use computer software which plots lines of best fit, or perhaps your grapical calculator.

C1 Which variables would you plot against each other to find the constants a and b in these equations? Say how you would obtain the values for a and b.

(a) $q = ap^2$ (b) $q^2 = ap^3$ (c) $q = \dfrac{a}{p^2} + b$ (d) $\dfrac{1}{q} = ap^2 + c$

C2 At the beginning of this century it was very common for statisticians to collect various pieces of data and attempt to fit equations to them. Here is some data gathered in 1922 showing height (x) and pulse rate (y) of some people. By transforming the data and drawing a line of best fit, find the value of a in the relationship $y = \dfrac{a}{\sqrt{x}}$.

Height, x (cm)	50	69·8	79·6	86·7	98·6	176·5
Pulse rate, y (counts per minute)	134	111	108	104	98	73

C3 Large tyres driven over rough ground tend to get very hot.

Here are some figures showing how the inside tyre temperatures of a large earthmover vary with the speed it is travelling.

Speed of earthmover (km/h)	5	10	25	30	40	50
Rise over air temperature (°C)	40	65	80	94	108	120

Make a rough sketch of temperature rise against speed. Use the sketch to help you decide on a possible relationship between temperature rise and speed.

By transforming the original data into a straight line, find the values of the constants in your formula.

What would you expect the rise in inside tyre temperature to be when the earthmover is travelling at 60 km/h?

C4 One of the most famous laws of planetary motion is called Kepler's third law. It was discovered in the 17th century by Johann Kepler. An approximate form of the law is:

> When a planet orbits a sun (or a moon orbits a planet) the square of the time to complete one orbit is proportional to the cube of the radius of its orbit.

Use the data below to investigate how well some of Jupiter's moons fit Kepler's third law.

Moon	Ganymede	Callisto	Leda	Himalia	Lysitha
Orbit radius (millions of km)	1·1	1·9	11·1	11·5	11·7
Time for one orbit (days)	7·2	16·9	239	251	259

C5 One of the advantages of the space shuttle is that the fuel tanks of the main rockets fall into the sea and can be reused if they are not damaged on impact.

A measure of the force on impact is the maximum deceleration felt by the body. This is measured as a multiple of acceleration due to gravity, $g\,\text{m/s}^2$.

Here are the results of some tests with models which investigated how the deceleration varied with impact speed onto water.

Impact speed on hitting water (m/s)	2	4	6	8	10
Maximum deceleration (g)	0·2	1·0	2·5	4·6	7·5

Transform this data into a straight line of best fit. Find the values of the constants in a formula connecting impact speed and maximum deceleration.

C6 Here are the figures showing average weekly household incomes and average weekly household expenditures on food in 1964.

Average weekly income (£s)	8·2	14·6	25·3	35·0	45·0	54·8	64·6	74·9	120·5
Average weekly expenditure on food (£s)	3·6	5·6	8·5	10·6	11·9	13·2	14·7	15·7	17·7

Find an empirical relationship between weekly income (x) and weekly expenditure on food (y) for these figures.

Option

According to Carol:

'Fitting a line of best fit can be made simpler if you use the following method.
Find the mean of the x-coordinates (m_x) and the mean of the y-coordinates (m_y). Then the line of best fit must go through the point (m_x, m_y).
This means that all you need to do now is tilt your ruler about this point to get the line of best fit.'

Is she correct? Investigate for some of the lines of best fit you have already drawn in this chapter.

Summary

- $y \propto x$ means that y is **directly** proportional to x (or $y = kx$, where k is a constant).

  $y \propto \dfrac{1}{x}$ means that y is **inversely** proportional to x (or $y = \dfrac{k}{x}$).

  Another common type of proportionality is the **inverse square**, $y \propto \dfrac{1}{x^2}$.

- A **line of best fit** is a straight line drawn by eye to pass as close to as many points as possible. Depending on the situation, it may go through the origin.

- It is possible to test the validity of many relationships by careful choice of axes and plotting points, and looking for a straight-line relationship. For example:

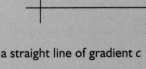

  (i) for $w = \dfrac{c}{v^2} + d$, plotting w against $\dfrac{1}{v^2}$ should give a straight line of gradient c and w-intercept d.

  (ii) for $r = kv^3$, plotting r against v^3 should give a straight line with a gradient of k and a zero r-intercept.

Mixed bag 2

1 The areas of the different faces of a cuboid are 24, 32 and 48 cm². Find the volume of the cuboid.

2 A number increased by 3 is a square number. The same number decreased by 3 gives the square root of the square number. What could the number be? Try to make up and test some similar puzzles.

3 What's wrong with this argument?

$$(^-x)^2 = (x)^2$$

Taking the square root of each side: $^-x = x$!

4 'The average person has a concentration span of 1 micro-century.' How long is this?

5 Many functions such as $\sqrt{x}$ and $\sin x$ have approximate formulas. Investigate how good these approximations are.
(For the trigonometric functions you will need to decide whether x is measured in radians or degrees.)

(a) $\sqrt{x} \approx a + \dfrac{x - a^2}{2a + 1}$ where a is an estimate of $\sqrt{x}$.

(b) $\tan x \approx \dfrac{10 + x}{100 - x}$ (c) $\sin x \approx x$

6 (a) Each of these equations and its inequality represent a line segment.

$$x = 2, \quad ^-1 \le y \le 1$$
$$y = 0, \quad 2 \le x \le 4$$
$$x = 4, \quad ^-1 \le y \le 1$$

The first one is shown on this grid.

The line segments join up to make a letter. Which letter?

(b) Which letter do these represent?

$$x = ^-5, \quad\quad ^-1 \le y \le 1; \quad\quad y = ^-x - 4, \quad ^-5 \le x \le ^-4$$
$$y = x + 4, \quad ^-4 \le x \le ^-3; \quad\quad x = ^-3, \quad\quad ^-1 \le y \le 1$$

7 Investigate this statement.

The sum of the absolute deviations of a set of figures is least when deviations are calculated from the median. Absolute deviation is the difference between two numbers ignoring the sign; for example, 6 − 14 is an absolute deviation of 8.

8   Imagine four 6-sided dice, A, B, C and D.
    Dice A has 4 on four faces and zero on two.
    Dice B has 3 on all its faces.
    Dice C has 2 on four faces and 6 on two.
    Dice D has 5 on three faces and 1 on the other three.

    Roy says that dice A will beat dice B about $\frac{2}{3}$ of the time and B will beat C
    about $\frac{2}{3}$ of the time, and so on.
    In other words, A beats B beats C beats D, all $\frac{2}{3}$ of the time.
    But D can beat A $\frac{2}{3}$ of the time!
    Is Roy correct? Investigate for yourself.

9   This is a very old card game.

    There are three cards: one black on one side, white on the other; one white
    both sides; one black both sides.

    The dealer shuffles the cards. One card is taken and placed on the table.
    The side showing is black.

    The dealer says, 'This is obviously cannot be the card which is white on both
    sides. So there is an equal chance that the card on the table is white or black
    on the other side.'

    Is the dealer telling the truth? Investigate.

10 What's wrong with these statements?

    (a) When tossing a coin, people call heads seven out of ten times, but heads
         will turn up only five times out of ten. So if you let your opponent do the
         calling, you have a much better chance of winning.

    (b) A sailor once put his head through a hole made in his ship by an enemy
         cannon ball. He said he would keep it there for the rest of the battle
         because it was extremely unlikely that another ball would come in exactly
         the same hole!

11 How could you test the truth of this statement?

    You are likely to make a correct weather forecast if you assume that
    tomorrow's weather will be like today's.

    If you can collect the necessary data, test the statement for yourself.

8 Angles and circles 2

A Technical terms – a review

You should have met some of these terms before, but they are listed here for completeness.

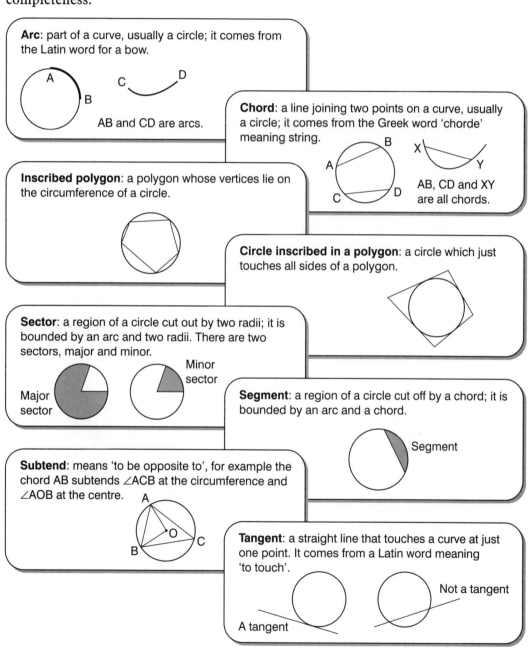

Arc: part of a curve, usually a circle; it comes from the Latin word for a bow.

AB and CD are arcs.

Chord: a line joining two points on a curve, usually a circle; it comes from the Greek word 'chorde' meaning string.

AB, CD and XY are all chords.

Inscribed polygon: a polygon whose vertices lie on the circumference of a circle.

Circle inscribed in a polygon: a circle which just touches all sides of a polygon.

Sector: a region of a circle cut out by two radii; it is bounded by an arc and two radii. There are two sectors, major and minor.

Major sector

Minor sector

Segment: a region of a circle cut off by a chord; it is bounded by an arc and a chord.

Segment

Subtend: means 'to be opposite to', for example the chord AB subtends ∠ACB at the circumference and ∠AOB at the centre.

Tangent: a straight line that touches a curve at just one point. It comes from a Latin word meaning 'to touch'.

A tangent

Not a tangent

A1 Can a chord of a circle ever be a line of symmetry?
Explain your answer.

A2 Imagine two points on a piece of paper.
Now imagine a circle which passes through both these points.
Imagine smaller and bigger circles that all pass through the two points.

(a) What path do the centres of these circles trace out?
Check your answer by drawing.

(b) What path (or paths) are traced out by the centres of circles which:
  (i) pass through a point and just touch a line
  (ii) just touch two lines
  (iii) pass through three points?

A3 Draw any triangle and then try to draw a circle which is inscribed in it.
(**Hint:** Think about symmetry!)

A4 Can you find a method to locate the mid-point of a circular arc?

A5 Two chords of a circle, AB and CD, cross at the point X.
By drawing and measuring, try to find a connection between the
product of the lengths AX and XB and the product of the lengths CX
and XD.

A6 Thirteenth-century Chinese
mathematicians were interested in
the properties of circles inscribed in
right-angled triangles.

Investigate, by drawing, the
relationship between the radius of
the inscribed circle and the
difference in length between the
hypotenuse and the sum of the
lengths of the other two sides.

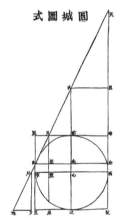

A7 Three circles cut two straight lines
as shown. The first circle cuts one
straight line at A and B, and the
other at A′ and B′.
The second circle cuts the first line
at B and C, and the second at B′ and
C′, and so on.

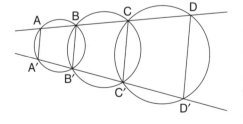

What do you notice about chords
AA′, BB′, CC′, …?

Try to prove your result.

B Tangents to a circle

AB is a chord of a circle, centre O.
OA and OB are radii of the circle.

X is the mid-point of the chord AB.

In triangles OAX and OBX:

OA = OB (they are both radii)
AX = XB (X is the mid-point of AB)

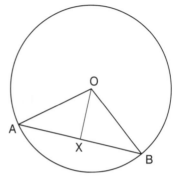

OX is common to both triangles.
So triangles OAX and OBX are congruent (SSS).

∠OXA and ∠OXB are corresponding angles, so
∠OXA = ∠OXB.

But the sum of these two angles is 180° (they make a straight line),
so ∠OXA and ∠OXB are both right-angles.

> The straight line which joins the centre of a circle to the mid-point of a chord (which is not a diameter) is perpendicular to the chord.
>
> Also, the straight line drawn from the centre of a circle perpendicular to the chord, bisects the chord.

It seems reasonable to *assume* that a tangent to a circle is perpendicular to the radius drawn through the point of contact. But we cannot be absolutely certain that this is true for every possible situation – we need to prove it.

TX is the tangent to a circle, centre O, and
OT is the radius at the point of contact.
Assume that ∠OTX is *not* 90°.

If this is true, it must be possible to draw a
line OA which is at right-angles to TX.
So ∠OAT = 90°.

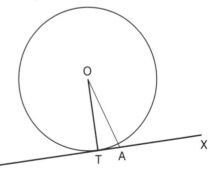

But if ∠OAT = 90° then OT is the hypotenuse
of the right-angled triangle OAT.

So OT > OA (the hypotenuse is always the
longest side).
But this means that A must be inside the circle
because the radius is OT.
But if A is inside the circle the line TA cuts the circle, which is impossible as
TA is a tangent.

So it is *impossible* for ∠OTX *not to be* 90°.
This means that ∠OTX must be 90°.

This method of proof is called **proof by contradiction**. You may have already
seen this type of proof on page 24.

B1 Calculate the angles marked with letters.
O is the centre of each circle and tangents touch each circle at T and U.

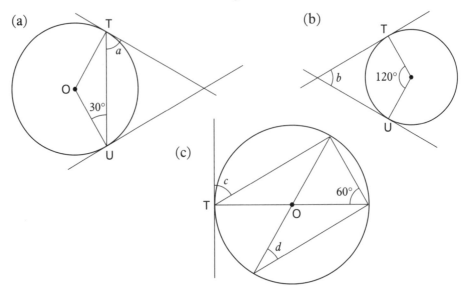

(a)

(b)

(c)

B2 T is a point outside a circle, centre O.
Tangents are drawn from T to the circle.
They touch the circle at the points A and B.

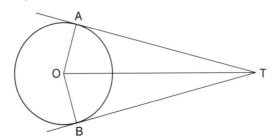

Prove that triangles OAT and OBT are congruent.
Don't forget to give a reason for each step in your argument.

What can you say about the lengths AT and BT?

What about ∠BTO and ∠ATO?

The results from the last question give three facts which are always true when tangents are drawn from the same point to a circle.

The tangents are equal in length.

They subtend equal angles at the centre of the circle.

They make equal angles with the straight line joining the point to the centre.

B3 Use one or more of the 'tangent facts' opposite to *prove* the answer to **A6**. You may find this diagram useful.

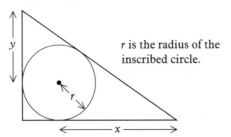

r is the radius of the inscribed circle.

B4 PT is a chord of a circle, centre O, AT a diameter and YTX a tangent.

Prove that ∠PTY = ∠TAP.

If A is allowed to move round the circumference so that TA is no longer a diameter of the circle, does ∠PTY still equal ∠TAP? Give a reason for your answer.

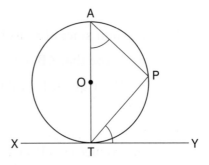

In this diagram, YX is a tangent touching the circle, centre O, at T. TP is a chord which divides the circle into two segments.

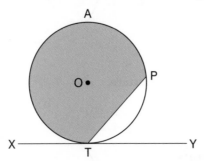

The shaded segment is called the **alternate segment** with respect to ∠PTY.

The result you should have found in the last part of **B4** is usually written as:

> The angle between a tangent and a chord drawn from the point of contact is equal to any angle subtended by the chord in the alternate segment.

⬤ *Thinking point*

The above fact is only true for angles in the alternate segment. Can you find a similar rule for angles in the other segment?

B5 Find the angles marked with letters.

(a)

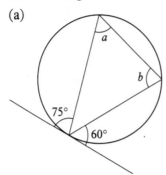

(b)

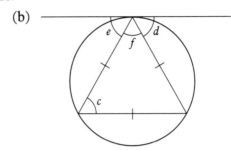

B6 The four sides of a quadrilateral ABCD are all tangents to a circle.

(a) Prove that AB + CD = BC + AD.

(b) If the quadrilateral is a parallelogram, prove that all four sides are equal.

B7 ABC is a triangle. AC is extended (or produced) to P, such that a tangent drawn from P touches the circle at B.

Prove that $\angle PCB = \angle ABP$.

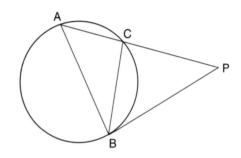

B8 Find the angles marked with letters.

(a)

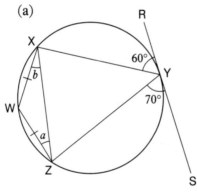

RS is a tangent.

(b)

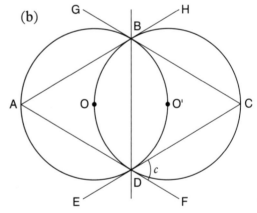

The two circles have the same radius. The centres are O and O', and AB, BC, CD and DA are tangents.

B9 Prove that quadrilateral ABCD is a rhombus.
The two circles are equal in size and cut each other's centres.
AB, BC, CD and DA are tangents.

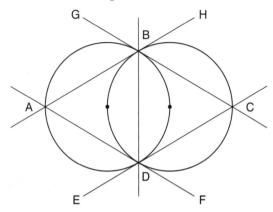

Summary

- The straight line which joins the centre of a circle to the mid-point of a chord (which is not a diameter) is perpendicular to the chord.

- The straight line drawn from the centre of a circle perpendicular to the chord, bisects the chord (AC = CB).

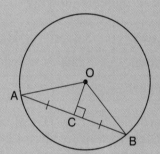

- When two tangents to a circle are drawn from the same point (E):

  - the tangents are equal in length (DE = FE)

  - they subtend equal angles at the centre of the circle (∠DOE = ∠FOE)

  - they make equal angles with the straight line joining the point to the centre (∠DEO = ∠FEO)

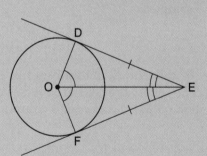

- The angle between a tangent and a chord (AB) drawn from the point of contact (A) is equal to the angle in the alternate segment (∠BAT = ∠ACB).

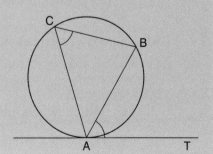

9 Introduction to matrices

A Starting matrices

A model car manufacturer has two factories, one in London and one in Glasgow.
Each factory makes three versions of the latest model – saloon, hatchback and estate.

Each month's production figures are recorded in a two-way table.
Here is an example showing the production figures for April.

Factory	Saloon	Hatchback	Estate
London	2200	1870	960
Glasgow	3510	1430	1250

If the order of the rows (London, Glasgow) and the order of the columns (Saloon,
Hatchback, Estate) are always kept the same, then each set of monthly production
figures can be summarised in a rectangular block (or **array**) of numbers. For
example:

$$\begin{bmatrix} 2200 & 1870 & 960 \\ 3510 & 1430 & 1250 \end{bmatrix}$$

We call a block of numbers like this a **matrix** (plural matrices).
The square brackets are used as a reminder to keep the array together.
Sometimes the rows and columns are labelled:

$$\begin{array}{c} \\ L \\ G \end{array} \begin{array}{ccc} S & H & E \\ \end{array}$$
$$\begin{array}{c} L \\ G \end{array} \begin{bmatrix} 2200 & 1870 & 960 \\ 3510 & 1430 & 1250 \end{bmatrix}$$

A1 Here is a matrix showing the production in May.

$$\begin{bmatrix} 4120 & 1200 & 800 \\ 3000 & 1563 & 1320 \end{bmatrix}$$

(a) Which factory made the most hatchbacks?

(b) How many estate cars did the London factory make?

(c) What was the total number of cars made in Glasgow?

The London factory made 2200 saloons in April and 4120 saloons in May. This makes a total of 6320 for the two months.

We can get similar totals from the other figures given in the two matrices.

In fact we can write those totals as a new matrix.

$$
\begin{array}{c}
\textbf{April} \\
\begin{array}{ccc}
\text{S} & \text{H} & \text{E}
\end{array} \\
\begin{array}{c}
\text{L} \\ \text{G}
\end{array}
\begin{bmatrix}
2200 & 1870 & 960 \\
3510 & 1430 & 1250
\end{bmatrix}
\end{array}
+
\begin{array}{c}
\textbf{May} \\
\begin{array}{ccc}
\text{S} & \text{H} & \text{E}
\end{array} \\
\begin{array}{c}
\text{L} \\ \text{G}
\end{array}
\begin{bmatrix}
4120 & 1200 & 800 \\
3000 & 1563 & 1320
\end{bmatrix}
\end{array}
=
\begin{array}{c}
\textbf{Total} \\
\begin{array}{ccc}
\text{S} & \text{H} & \text{E}
\end{array} \\
\begin{array}{c}
\text{L} \\ \text{G}
\end{array}
\begin{bmatrix}
6320 & 3070 & 1760 \\
6510 & 2993 & 2570
\end{bmatrix}
\end{array}
$$

A2 This matrix shows the expected production figures for August.

$$
\begin{bmatrix}
6000 & 0 & 0 \\
0 & 500 & 0
\end{bmatrix}
$$

Explain what you think happens in August.

A3 A record shop classifies its stock into four categories:

Pop, Jazz, Easy Listening and Classical.

Each day the shop notes the number of records, cassettes and CDs sold in each category.

Here are the matrices for Monday's and Tuesday's sales:

$$
\begin{array}{c}
\textbf{Monday} \\
\begin{array}{ccc}
\text{R} & \text{Cass} & \text{CD}
\end{array} \\
\begin{array}{c}
\text{Pop} \\ \text{Jazz} \\ \text{EL} \\ \text{Class}
\end{array}
\begin{bmatrix}
7 & 24 & 76 \\
3 & 21 & 18 \\
0 & 34 & 21 \\
2 & 8 & 38
\end{bmatrix}
\end{array}
\qquad
\begin{array}{c}
\textbf{Tuesday} \\
\begin{array}{ccc}
\text{R} & \text{Cass} & \text{CD}
\end{array} \\
\begin{array}{c}
\text{Pop} \\ \text{Jazz} \\ \text{EL} \\ \text{Class}
\end{array}
\begin{bmatrix}
8 & 26 & 70 \\
5 & 18 & 0 \\
1 & 34 & 30 \\
3 & 0 & 20
\end{bmatrix}
\end{array}
$$

(a) Write down the matrix which represents the combined sales for Monday and Tuesday.

(b) What do you think the matrix below on the right represents?

$$
\begin{array}{c}
\begin{array}{ccc}
\text{R} & \text{Cass} & \text{CD}
\end{array} \\
\begin{array}{c}
\text{Pop} \\ \text{Jazz} \\ \text{EL} \\ \text{Class}
\end{array}
\begin{bmatrix}
7 & 24 & 76 \\
3 & 21 & 18 \\
0 & 34 & 21 \\
2 & 8 & 38
\end{bmatrix}
\end{array}
-
\begin{array}{c}
\begin{array}{ccc}
\text{R} & \text{Cass} & \text{CD}
\end{array} \\
\begin{array}{c}
\text{Pop} \\ \text{Jazz} \\ \text{EL} \\ \text{Class}
\end{array}
\begin{bmatrix}
8 & 26 & 70 \\
5 & 18 & 0 \\
1 & 34 & 30 \\
3 & 0 & 20
\end{bmatrix}
\end{array}
=
\begin{array}{c}
\begin{array}{ccc}
\text{R} & \text{Cass} & \text{CD}
\end{array} \\
\begin{array}{c}
\text{Pop} \\ \text{Jazz} \\ \text{EL} \\ \text{Class}
\end{array}
\begin{bmatrix}
-1 & -2 & 6 \\
-2 & 3 & 18 \\
-1 & 0 & -9 \\
-1 & 8 & 18
\end{bmatrix}
\end{array}
$$

(c) By a fluke, sales on Saturday were exactly double those on Monday. Write down the matrix representing the sales figures for Saturday.

In the case of the model car manufacturer, monthly figures were represented in a matrix with two rows and three columns.

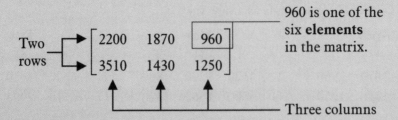

960 is one of the six **elements** in the matrix.

Two rows

Three columns

We say that the matrix is a 2 × 3 (**two by three**) matrix, and that it has **dimensions** 2 × 3.

Dimensions of a matrix are always given as:

(the number of rows)   by   (the number of columns).

A 4 × 5 matrix has 20 elements, a 7 × 3 has 21 elements, and so on.

It is often convenient to use a single letter to represent a matrix.
We write a squiggle under the letter. This shows that it stands for a matrix and not a single number.

Suppose M stands for the matrix representing Monday's sales in the record shop and T stands for the matrix giving Tuesday's sales.

We calculate $M + T$ to find the matrix representing the total sales for these two days.

A4   What do you think the matrix $T - M$ represents?

A5   (a) Calculate $M + M$.

(b) Write down the matrix represented by $2M$.

A6   Calculate $\frac{1}{2}(M + T)$. What might this matrix represent?

The company making model cars wants to increase its production for June by 20% on that for May. To find these figures we need to multiply May's figures by 1·2.

If May's figures are represented by the matrix M, where

$$M = \begin{bmatrix} 4120 & 1200 & 800 \\ 3000 & 1563 & 1320 \end{bmatrix},$$

then June's figures will be $1 \cdot 2M = \begin{bmatrix} 4944 & 1440 & 960 \\ 3600 & 1876 & 1584 \end{bmatrix}$.

Suppose A and B are both 2×3 matrices,

where $A = \begin{bmatrix} 1 & 0 & 2 \\ 4 & 2 & 6 \end{bmatrix}$ and $B = \begin{bmatrix} 2 & 4 & 0 \\ 4 & 0 & 4 \end{bmatrix}$.

A7   Calculate $A + B$ and $A - B$.

A8   For the matrices A and B above, write down the matrices represented by

(a) $2A$ (b) $2A + B$ (c) $B - A$

A9   Write down two 2×3 matrices of your own.
Label these matrices X and Y.
Write down matrices represented by:

(a) $X + Y$ (b) $X - Y$ (c) $X + 2Y$ (d) $X - 2Y$

Did you know?

The Ancient Chinese used counting boards to help them with calculations.

These boards were divided up into squares and numbers represented by rods placed in them.

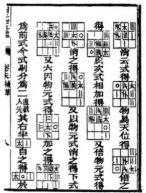

Almost 2000 years ago the Chinese had the idea of using these squares for holding information – very much like the elements of a modern matrix.

B Matrix multiplication

This matrix gives the contents of two different breakfast menus in a nursing home.

	Pots of yoghurt	Slices of bread	Pats of butter	Portions of cheese
Menu A	1	3	3	2
Menu B	0	4	2	3

It could be called a Menu/Food matrix.

Each food (yoghurt, bread, butter and cheese) contains different amounts of protein, fat and carbohydrate. These are the nutritional values.

In the matrix below, the foods are shown in the rows and the nutritional values in the columns. It is called a Food/Nutrition matrix.

Nutrition

		Protein (g)	Fat (g)	Carbohydrate (g)
Food	Pot of yoghurt	6·0	1·0	20·0
	Slice of bread	1·6	0·4	13·7
	Pat of butter	0·1	5·0	0
	Portion of cheese	6·0	7·0	0·5

B1 (a) Calculate the amount of:

(i) protein in menu A   (ii) protein in menu B

(iii) fat in menu A   (iv) fat in menu B

(b) Make a Menu/Nutrition matrix as shown below.
Fill in the matrix – your answers to (a) will help you start.

	Protein (g)	Fat (g)	Carbohydrate (g)
Menu A			
Menu B			

92

Here are the Menu/Food and the Food/Nutrition matrices set out side by side.

		Menu/Food		
	Pots of yoghurt	Slices of bread	Pats of butter	Portions of cheese
Menu A	1	3	3	2
Menu B	0	4	2	3

		Food/Nutrition	
	Protein (g)	Fat (g)	Carbohydrate (g)
Pot of yoghurt	6·0	1·0	20·0
Slice of bread	1·6	0·4	13·7
Pat of butter	0·1	5·0	0
Portion of cheese	6·0	7·0	0·5

To find the amount of protein in menu A, you take the row for menu A in the first matrix and the column for protein in the second matrix and work out:

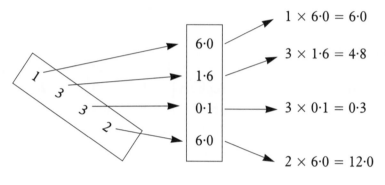

$1 \times 6·0 = 6·0$ 1 yoghurt with 6 g of protein

$3 \times 1·6 = 4·8$ 3 slices of bread each containing 1·6 g of protein

$3 \times 0·1 = 0·3$ 3 pats of butter each containing 0·1 g of protein

$2 \times 6·0 = 12·0$ 2 portions of cheese each containing 6 g of protein

So the total protein content in menu A is

$6·0 + 4·8 + 0·3 + 12·0 = \mathbf{23·1\,g}$.

This figure can be entered into the menu A row and the protein column of the Menu/Nutrition matrix.

	Protein (g)	Fat (g)	Carbohydrate (g)
Menu A	23·1		
Menu B			

Other elements in the Menu/Nutrition matrix may be calculated in a similar way. For example, to find the amount of fat in menu B:

		Menu/Food		
	Yoghurt	Bread	Butter	Cheese
Menu A	1	3	3	2
Menu B	0	4	2	3

	Food/Nutrition		
	Protein	Fat	Carbohydrate
Yoghurt	6·0	1·0	20·0
Bread	1·6	0·4	13·7
Butter	0·1	5·0	0
Cheese	6·0	7·0	0·5

The fat in menu B $= (0 \times 1·0) + (4 \times 0·4) + (2 \times 5·0) + (3 \times 7·0) = 32·6\,g$.

B2 What do each of the following give, if in each case you 'Go across the row and down the column, multiplying pairs and adding as you go'? Check your answers against your answers to **B1**.

(a)　　　Menu/Food

Food/Nutrition

	Yoghurt	Bread	Butter	Cheese
Menu A	1	3	3	2
Menu B	0	4	2	3

	Protein	Fat	Carbohydrate
Yoghurt	6·0	1·0	20·0
Bread	1·6	0·4	13·7
Butter	0·1	5·0	0
Cheese	6·0	7·0	0·5

(b)　　　Menu/Food

Food/Nutrition

	Yoghurt	Bread	Butter	Cheese
Menu A	1	3	3	2
Menu B	0	4	2	3

	Protein	Fat	Carbohydrate
Yoghurt	6·0	1·0	20·0
Bread	1·6	0·4	13·7
Butter	0·1	5·0	0
Cheese	6·0	7·0	0·5

The advantage of calculating the nutritional value for each menu in this way is that it is a systematic method. The same method could be used for a far larger number of menus. However, in this case a computer would probably be used. Computers need a systematic method.

In this way a large number of different menus could be investigated in order to match a menu with a particular person's needs.

The completed matrix is called the **product** of the Menu/Food and the Food/Nutrition matrices.

To obtain this we have to perform **matrix multiplication**. As you have probably noticed already, matrix multiplication is not performed in the same way as 'normal' multiplication.

There is no special symbol for the multiplication of matrices. We just place them side by side, as shown here.

$$\begin{bmatrix} 1 & 3 & 3 & 2 \\ 0 & 4 & 2 & 3 \end{bmatrix} \begin{bmatrix} 6·0 & 1·0 & 20·0 \\ 1·6 & 0·4 & 13·7 \\ 0·1 & 5·0 & 0 \\ 6·0 & 7·0 & 0·5 \end{bmatrix} = \begin{bmatrix} 23·1 & 31·2 & 62·1 \\ 24·6 & 32·6 & 56·3 \end{bmatrix}$$

Here is another matrix multiplication, this time with simpler numbers.

$$
\begin{bmatrix} 1 & 0 & 2 \\ 0 & 1 & 2 \end{bmatrix}
\begin{bmatrix} 2 & 1 & 2 & 0 \\ 3 & 0 & 1 & 2 \\ 1 & 2 & 1 & 1 \end{bmatrix}
=
\begin{bmatrix} 4 & 5 & 4 & 2 \\ 5 & 4 & 3 & 4 \end{bmatrix}
$$

Make sure that you agree with the answer!

There are several important points about matrix multiplication:

- The number of **columns** in the first matrix must equal the number of **rows** in the second.

- The number of rows in the product matrix is equal to the number of rows in the first matrix.

- The number of columns in the product matrix is equal to the number of columns in the second matrix.

- When multiplying matrices there is a simple 'chain rule' which must be observed.

  [First matrix a by $\boxed{b}$] [Second matrix $\boxed{b}$ by c] = [Product matrix a by c]

  For example, a 7×3 matrix multiplied by a 3×2 matrix gives a 7×2 matrix.

  The numbers in boxes must be the same. You cannot multiply a 3×2 matrix by a 3×3 matrix.

B3 Write down which additions and multiplications can be done with the matrices $\underset{\sim}{A}$, $\underset{\sim}{B}$, $\underset{\sim}{C}$ and $\underset{\sim}{D}$, if:

$\underset{\sim}{A}$ is 2×3, $\underset{\sim}{B}$ is 2×2, $\underset{\sim}{C}$ is 3×2 and $\underset{\sim}{D}$ is 2×3.

B4 Copy and complete these matrix products.

(a) $\begin{bmatrix} 1 & 0 \\ 0 & 1 \end{bmatrix} \begin{bmatrix} 1 & 2 & 1 \\ 3 & 4 & 1 \end{bmatrix} = \begin{bmatrix} 1 & ? & 1 \\ ? & ? & 1 \end{bmatrix}$

(b) $\begin{bmatrix} 1 & 2 \\ 2 & 1 \end{bmatrix} \begin{bmatrix} 1 & 2 \\ 2 & 1 \end{bmatrix} = \begin{bmatrix} 5 & ? \\ ? & 5 \end{bmatrix}$

(c) $\begin{bmatrix} 1 & 1 \\ 2 & 1 \end{bmatrix} \begin{bmatrix} 2 & 1 & 3 \\ 3 & 1 & 2 \end{bmatrix} = \begin{bmatrix} 5 & 2 & 5 \\ ? & ? & ? \end{bmatrix}$

(d) $\begin{bmatrix} 1 & 0 & 0 \\ 1 & 0 & 1 \\ 1 & 1 & 1 \end{bmatrix} \begin{bmatrix} 1 & 2 \\ 2 & 1 \\ 1 & 1 \end{bmatrix} = \begin{bmatrix} 1 & ? \\ 2 & ? \\ 4 & ? \end{bmatrix}$

B5 Make up some matrix multiplications of your own where the first multiplying matrix is $\begin{bmatrix} 1 & 0 \\ 0 & 1 \end{bmatrix}$. What do you notice?

B6 What effect does multiplication by $\begin{bmatrix} 2 & 0 \\ 0 & 2 \end{bmatrix}$ have on a matrix?

B7 Jean says that it is impossible to square a 2×3 matrix.
Is she correct? Give a reason or example to support your answer.

B8 Is this matrix calculation correct? Explain your answer.

$$\underset{\sim}{A} = \begin{bmatrix} 2 & 4 \\ 1 & 3 \end{bmatrix} \text{ so } \underset{\sim}{A}\underset{\sim}{A} \text{ or } \underset{\sim}{A}^2 = \begin{bmatrix} 2^2 & 4^2 \\ 1^2 & 3^2 \end{bmatrix} = \begin{bmatrix} 4 & 16 \\ 1 & 9 \end{bmatrix}$$

B9 Write down at least two matrix products whose answer is [1].

B10 When numbers are multiplied together, the order does not matter so, for example, 5×3 gives the same as 3×5.
Is this also true for matrix products?
Give some examples to support your answer.

Here is how a Chinese mathematician would have used the 'method of tables' to solve simultaneous equations, in which numbers are held in compartments (just like modern matrices).
The simultaneous equations to be solved are $4x + y = 13$ and $x + 2y = 5$.

First the equations are put into 'matrix form': $\begin{bmatrix} 4 & 1 \\ 1 & 2 \\ 13 & 5 \end{bmatrix}$.

The second column is multiplied by 4, subtracted from the first column, and the result put into the second column: $\begin{bmatrix} 4 & 0 \\ 1 & ^-7 \\ 13 & ^-7 \end{bmatrix}$.

Multiply the first column by 7, add the result to the second column and write the answer in the first column: $\begin{bmatrix} 28 & 0 \\ 0 & ^-7 \\ 84 & ^-7 \end{bmatrix}$.

This shows that $28x = 84$ or $x = 3$, and $^-7y = ^-7$ or $y = 1$.

B11 Use the method of tables to solve these simultaneous equations.

(a) $2x + y = 3$, $x + y = 2$

(b) $2x + 3y = 5$, $x + y = 1$

The aim is to put a zero in the top right-hand corner and in the middle row on the left-hand side. What are the advantages of doing this?

Options

Spreadsheets may be used to perform matrix multiplication.
A sample set of formulas and the corresponding results are shown below.

It shows the matrix product $\begin{bmatrix} 0 & 1 \\ 1 & 0 \end{bmatrix}\begin{bmatrix} -9 & 3 & 3 \\ 1 & 2 & 3 \end{bmatrix}$.

	A	B	C	D	E	F
1						
2						
3	0	1		-9	3	3
4	1	0		1	2	3
5						
6			=A3*D3+B3*D4	=A3*E3+B3*E4	=A3*F3+B3*F4	
7			=A4*D3+B4*D4	=A4*E3+B4*E4	=A4*F3+B4*F4	

A

	A	B	C	D	E	F
1						
2						
3	0	1		-9	3	3
4	1	0		1	2	3
5						
6			1	2	3	
7			-9	3	3	

- Adapt the coding so that the spreadsheet is able to calculate the product of 2×2 matrices.

  Use your spreadsheet or graphical calculator to investigate the effects of multiplying matrices by

$$\begin{bmatrix} 0 & 1 \\ 1 & 0 \end{bmatrix}, \begin{bmatrix} 1 & 0 \\ 1 & 0 \end{bmatrix}, \begin{bmatrix} 0 & 1 \\ 0 & 1 \end{bmatrix} \text{ or } \begin{bmatrix} 2 & 2 \\ 2 & 2 \end{bmatrix}.$$

  Make a note of anything interesting you find.

- Alter the spreadsheet so that it is able to calculate the product of a 2×4 and a 4×3 matrix. Use it to check your answers to **B1**.

Summary

- Matrices are rectangular blocks of numbers which can be used to store information. For example,

$$A = \begin{bmatrix} 1 & 16 & 0 \\ 2 & ^-3 & 4 \end{bmatrix}$$ is a matrix with two rows and three columns.

Each number in the matrix is called an **element** – this matrix has six elements.

The shape or **dimension** of a matrix is given as:

(the number of **rows**) by (the number of **columns**),

so A is a 2 × 3 matrix.

- Two matrices can be added (or their differences found) if they have the same dimensions. The resulting matrix is found by adding (or subtracting) corresponding elements:

$$\begin{bmatrix} 1 & ^-2 \\ 3 & 0 \end{bmatrix} + \begin{bmatrix} 2 & 4 \\ ^-1 & 4 \end{bmatrix} = \begin{bmatrix} 1+2 & ^-2+4 \\ 3-1 & 0+4 \end{bmatrix} = \begin{bmatrix} 3 & 2 \\ 2 & 4 \end{bmatrix}$$

However, this calculation is meaningless:

$$\begin{bmatrix} 1 & 0 \\ 2 & ^-2 \end{bmatrix} + \begin{bmatrix} 6 & 6 & 1 \\ 8 & 2 & 0 \end{bmatrix}$$

- Calculating the product of two matrices is only possible if the number of columns in the left matrix is equal to the number of rows in the right matrix.

$$\begin{bmatrix} 1 & 3 \\ 2 & 0 \\ ^-2 & 4 \end{bmatrix}\begin{bmatrix} 3 & 0 \\ 5 & ^-1 \end{bmatrix} = \begin{bmatrix} (1 \times 3)+(3 \times 5) & (1 \times 0)+(3 \times ^-1) \\ (2 \times 3)+(0 \times 5) & (2 \times 0)+(0 \times ^-1) \\ (^-2 \times 3)+(4 \times 5) & (^-2 \times 0)+(4 \times ^-1) \end{bmatrix} = \begin{bmatrix} 18 & ^-3 \\ 6 & 0 \\ 14 & ^-4 \end{bmatrix}$$

This product cannot be defined:

$$\begin{bmatrix} 1 & 7 \\ 0 & 2 \end{bmatrix}\begin{bmatrix} ^-2 & 5 \\ 4 & 0 \\ 1 & ^-4 \end{bmatrix} \quad \text{(a 2 × 2 with a 3 × 2 matrix)}$$

10 Iterative solution of equations

A graphical calculator or spreadsheet will be useful for this chapter.

A Iterative formulas and equations

A1 Copy and complete this table.
(Your answers may differ slightly in the last digit, due to rounding.)

Iterative formula	u_1	u_2	u_3	u_4	u_5	u_6
(a) $u_{n+1} = u_n + 7$	7			28		42
(b) $u_{n+1} = \dfrac{u_n}{2} + 1$	2		2			2
(c) $u_{n+1} = \dfrac{1}{u_n} + 1$	4	1·25			1·642 857 1	
(d) $u_{n+1} = \sqrt{(u_n + 7)}$	3		3·187 832 8			

(e) Which of the sequences seem to approach (converge to) a limit?

A2 (a) Solve the equation $x = \dfrac{x + 18}{4}$.

(b) What value does the sequence $u_{n+1} = \dfrac{u_n + 18}{4}$ converge to when $u_1 = 10$?

(c) What seems to be the connection between your two answers?

This spreadsheet shows the first few terms in the sequence $u_{n+1} = \dfrac{u_n + 8}{3}$ with $u_1 = 6$. (It also shows the formulas needed to produce these values.)

	A	B
1	Term	Value
2	1	6
3	=A2+1	=(B2+8)/3
4	=A3+1	=(B3+8)/3

	A	B
	Term	Value
1		6
2		4.6666666667
4	3	4.2222222222

A3 (a) Use the iterative formula $u_{n+1} = \dfrac{u_n + 8}{3}$ to generate a sequence starting with $u_1 = 6$. Calculate enough terms to be confident that the sequence converges to a limit.

(b) Solve the equation $x = \dfrac{x + 8}{3}$.

(c) What do you think is the connection between the solution to (b) and the limit of the sequence $u_{n+1} = \dfrac{u_n + 8}{3}$ when $u_1 = 6$?

It can sometimes take a large number of terms to see if a particular iterative formula does converge. Even then you cannot be absolutely certain. Many sequences seem to converge at first but then act rather strangely. Some of these 'strange' sequences are dealt with in *Book YX2*.

A4 Some formulas and the values for an iteration from a spreadsheet are shown below.

	A	B
1	Term	Value
2	1	3
3	=A2+1	=(B2+20)/2
4	=A3+1	=(B3+20)/2
5	=A4+1	=(B4+20)/2
6	=A5+1	

	A	B
1	Term	Value
2	1	3
3	2	11.5
		15.75
		17.875
		18.9375

	A	B
	Term	Value
57	56	19.9999999999999995
58	57	19.9999999999999998
59	58	19.9999999999999999
60	59	19.9999999999999999
61	60	20
62	61	20

(a) What is the value of the first term in the sequence?

(b) Write down the iterative formula for the sequence.

(c) What appears to be the limit of the sequence?

Once a sequence has begun to converge, by definition the terms approach a certain value (the limit). We say that the terms **tend to a limiting value**. If this limiting value is represented by x, then:

both u_{n+1} and u_n are approximately equal to x, when n is large.

This means, for example, that the iterative formula $u_{n+1} = \dfrac{u_n + 8}{3}$ gives the limiting value $x = \dfrac{x + 8}{3}$.

Therefore the solution to the equation $x = \dfrac{x + 8}{3}$ is the limiting value of the iterative formula $u_{n+1} = \dfrac{u_n + 8}{3}$.

Look back at **A2** and **A3** to check that you understand this.

A5 It appears from **A3** that the equation $x = \dfrac{x + 8}{3}$ can be solved

by finding the limit of the iterative formula $u_{n+1} = \dfrac{u_n + 8}{3}$ with

$u_1 = 6$. But what about for other values of u_1?

Experiment with a few different values of u_1. What do you find? You may find it useful to pool your results with a partner.

Most graphical or programmable calculators can be used to work out the terms of an iterative sequence. Here are the key strokes which work for many machines. Yours might be slightly different – look in the manual!

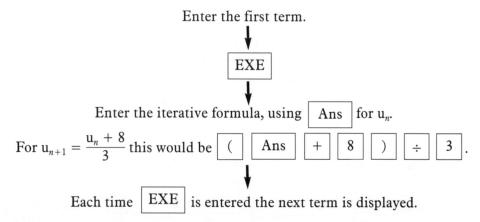

Enter the first term.

↓

EXE

↓

Enter the iterative formula, using $\boxed{\text{Ans}}$ for u_n.

For $u_{n+1} = \dfrac{u_n + 8}{3}$ this would be $\boxed{(}\ \boxed{\text{Ans}}\ \boxed{+}\ \boxed{8}\ \boxed{)}\ \boxed{\div}\ \boxed{3}$.

↓

Each time $\boxed{\text{EXE}}$ is entered the next term is displayed.

Experiment with your own machine by checking some of your answers in this section.

A6 Here is a simple BASIC program for calculating the terms of iterative sequences.

```
10 INPUT "First term";T
20 INPUT "Number of terms";N
30 FOR J=1 TO N
40 PRINT J,T
50 NT=(2*T-3)/5
60 T=NT
70 NEXT J
```

Write down the iterative formula which line 50 uses.

A7 Find which of these equations may be solved using the given iterative formula. Choose your own starting value (u_1). Make a note of anything interesting you find.

(a) $x = \dfrac{x - 2}{3}$ $\qquad u_{n+1} = \dfrac{u_n - 2}{3}$

(b) $x = \dfrac{x + 2}{5}$ $\qquad u_{n+1} = \dfrac{u_n + 2}{5}$

(c) $x = \dfrac{2x - 2}{3}$ $\qquad u_{n+1} = \dfrac{2u_n - 2}{3}$

101

B Iteration and quadratic equations

Iterative formulas may be used to solve equations other than the very simple ones in the last section. In fact solving an equation like $x = \dfrac{x+2}{2}$ is probably best done using algebra! However, as you found in chapter 5, some equations are very difficult or even impossible to solve by algebra. Iteration can come in very useful in giving accurate solutions to these.

If the equation $x = \dfrac{10}{x+2}$ needs to be solved, we can use the iterative

formula $u_{n+1} = \dfrac{10}{u_n + 2}$.

Here are the first few terms:

	A		B
1	Term		Value
2		1	2.0000
3		2	2.5000
4		3	2.2222
5		4	2.3684
		5	2.2892

	A		B
1	Term		Value
2		1	=2
3		=A2+1	=10/(B2+2)
4		=A3+1	=10/(B3+2)
5		=A4+1	=10/(B4+2)

	A	B
15	14	2.3167
16	15	2.3166
17	16	2.3167
18	17	2.3166
19	18	2.3166
20	19	2.3166
21	20	2.3166
22	21	2.3166
23	22	2.3166
24	23	2.3166
25	24	2.3166
26	25	2.3166

These spreadsheet results (which are correct to 4 decimal places) suggest very strongly that the sequence converges $(u_n \approx u_{n+1})$ to the value of 2·3166.

So the solution to the equation $x = \dfrac{10}{x+2}$ $(x \approx u_n)$ is 2·3166 correct to 4 d.p.

B1 The equation $x = \dfrac{10}{x+2}$ can be rearranged to give $x(x+2) = 10$.

Show that $x = 2·317$ is a good approximate solution to this equation.

B2 Use the iterative formula $u_{n+1} = \dfrac{5}{u_n + 2}$ with $u_1 = 1$ to generate a

sequence. Find the limit of this sequence to 2 decimal places. Check that this limit approximately satisfies the equation $x(x+2) = 5$.

B3 Which of these are correct rearrangements of $x^2 - 5x + 2 = 0$?

(a) $x = \dfrac{x^2 - 5}{2}$ (b) $x = \dfrac{x^2 + 2}{5}$ (c) $x = 5 - \dfrac{2}{x}$ (d) $x = \sqrt{(2 + 5x)}$

B4 (a) Find the limit, correct to 2 d.p., of the sequence which is described by the iterative formula $u_{n+1} = \dfrac{1}{u_n} + 2$ and begins $u_1 = 2$.

(b) Show that the answer to (a) is an approximate solution to the equation $x^2 - 2x - 1 = 0$.

B5 A solution to the equation $x = \dfrac{x^3 + 1}{3}$ lies between $^{-}1{\cdot}5$ and $1{\cdot}5$.

(a) Use the iterative formula $u_{n+1} = \dfrac{u_n^3 + 1}{3}$ to find an approximate solution to the equation correct to 2 d.p.

(b) Check your answer by substituting this value back into the original equation.

To solve the equation $x = \dfrac{5}{x + 3}$, try using the iterative formula $u_{n+1} = \dfrac{5}{u_n + 3}$.

It is easy to write down the iterative formula because the original equation is in the form $x = $ (**an expression containing** x).

We say that x is equal to a **function** of x and write $x = f(x)$.

Simply replace the x on the left-hand side by u_{n+1}, and the x on the right-hand side by u_n. So the first task in trying to solve an equation using iteration is to rearrange it in this form.

For example, suppose you want to solve the equation $x(x + 1) = 6$.
You can rearrange it by dividing both sides by $(x + 1)$.

This gives $x = \dfrac{6}{x + 1}$, so an iterative formula is $u_{n+1} = \dfrac{6}{u_n + 1}$.

B6 (a) Rearrange the formula $x(x + 3) = 20$ into the form $x = f(x)$.

(b) Write down the corresponding iterative formula.

(c) Use the iterative formula to generate a sequence, starting with $u_1 = 3$. Continue until you can write down the limit correct to 2 decimal places.

(d) Check that this limit approximately satisfies the equation $x(x + 3) = 20$.

Sometimes it may take several steps to rearrange an equation into the form $x = f(x)$. For example, take $x^2 + 2x - 5 = 0$:

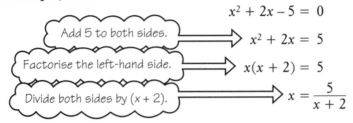

$$x^2 + 2x - 5 = 0$$

Add 5 to both sides. → $x^2 + 2x = 5$

Factorise the left-hand side. → $x(x + 2) = 5$

Divide both sides by $(x + 2)$. → $x = \dfrac{5}{x + 2}$

B7 Use the result above to write down an iterative formula to solve the quadratic equation $x^2 + 2x - 5 = 0$.

Use it to find a solution to the quadratic equation to 2 d.p. You will need to choose your own value of u_1.

Check your answer by substituting your solution back into the equation.

B8 (a) Show that the equation $x^2 - 3x - 5 = 0$ can be written in the form $x = \dfrac{5}{x - 3}$.

(b) Write down the corresponding iterative formula.

(c) Choose your own value of u_1 and use the iterative formula to solve $x^2 - 3x - 5 = 0$, correct to 2 d.p.

(d) Check that your solution approximately satisfies the equation $x^2 - 3x - 5 = 0$.

B9 The equation $x^2 + x - 42 = 0$ can be solved by factorising.

$$x^2 + x - 42 = (x - 6)(x + 7)$$
$$(x - 6)(x + 7) = 0$$
So either $x - 6 = 0$ or $x + 7 = 0$
So either $x = 6$ or $x = {}^-7$
The solutions are 6 and $^-7$.

Can you find *both* these solutions by iteration?

Investigate this and write down anything interesting you observe.

◢Challenge

The general quadratic equation may be written $x^2 + ax + b = 0$, where a and b are numbers. So for the equation $x^2 - x + 4 = 0$, $a = {}^-1$ and $b = 4$.

Rearrange the general quadratic in the form $x = f(x)$.

Use your rearrangement to write down an iterative formula for solving the quadratic equation $x^2 + ax + b = 0$.

Experiment to see how useful the iterative method is for different values of a and b. Make a note of anything useful you find.

c Bugs

C1 (a) Show that the equation $x^2 + x - 5 = 0$ can be rewritten as $x = 5 - x^2$ (so that $x = f(x)$).

(b) The corresponding iterative formula is $u_{n+1} = 5 - u_n{}^2$. Can you use it to solve $x^2 + x - 5 = 0$? Experiment with different values of u_1.

Not all iterative formulas based on equations rearranged into the form $x = f(x)$ give a solution to the original equation.

The equation $x^2 + 2x - 15 = 0$ can be rearranged in several ways to give $x = f(x)$. Make sure you understand each method.

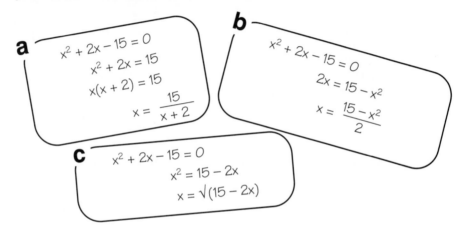

a
$$x^2 + 2x - 15 = 0$$
$$x^2 + 2x = 15$$
$$x(x + 2) = 15$$
$$x = \frac{15}{x + 2}$$

b
$$x^2 + 2x - 15 = 0$$
$$2x = 15 - x^2$$
$$x = \frac{15 - x^2}{2}$$

c
$$x^2 + 2x - 15 = 0$$
$$x^2 = 15 - 2x$$
$$x = \sqrt{(15 - 2x)}$$

C2 Write down the iterative formula for each of the three arrangements above.

(a) Which of the iterative formulas converge to a limit?

(b) Use the one (or ones) which converge to solve $x^2 + 2x - 15 = 0$.

(c) Compare your answers to (b) with the solutions arrived at by factorising $x^2 + 2x - 15$.

Another problem arises when an equation has more than one solution. An iterative formula may lead to one of the solutions but not to the other. A different iterative formula may be needed to get the second solution.

C3 The graph of $y = x^2 + x - 4$ shows that there is a solution of the equation $x^2 + x - 4 = 0$ close to 1·6 and another close to ⁻2·6.

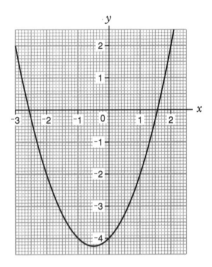

(a) Which one(s) will the iterative formula corresponding to

$$x = \frac{4}{x + 1} \text{ give?}$$

(b) Show how $x = \dfrac{4}{x} - 1$ can be formed from $x^2 + x - 4 = 0$.

(c) Use the iterative formula based on (b) to find the solution(s) to $x^2 + x - 4 = 0$.

C4 Arrange the equation $x^2 - 10x + 3 = 0$ in the form $x = \dfrac{x^2 + a}{b}$, where a and b are constants. Use iteration to find a root of this equation to an accuracy of 2 decimal places. Investigate what happens when (a) $u_1 = 0$ (b) $u_1 = 5$ and (c) $u_1 = 10$.

C5 The equation $x(x + 2) = 5$ has a solution close to 1·5 and another close to ⁻3·5.

Use iterative formulas to find both solutions correct to 2 d.p.

C6 Here are three ways to rearrange $x^3 = 10$.

a

$$x^3 = 10$$

Divide both sides by x: $\quad x^2 = \dfrac{10}{x}$

Take the square root of both sides: $\quad x = \sqrt{\dfrac{10}{x}}$

b

$$x^3 = 10$$

Divide both sides by x^2: $\quad x = \dfrac{10}{x^2}$

c

$$x^3 = 10$$

Multiply both sides by x: $\qquad\qquad\qquad\qquad\qquad x^4 = 10x$

Take the square root of both sides: $\qquad\qquad\quad x^2 = \sqrt{(10x)}$

Take the square root of both sides again: $\quad x = \sqrt{(\sqrt{(10x)})}$

For each one write down the corresponding iterative formula.
Starting in each case with $u_1 = 2$, use each iterative formula to solve $x^3 = 10$. What do you notice?

D Take your pick

> An equation of the form $f(x) = k$ can be solved by:
> - an algebraic method if $f(x)$ is simple enough.
> - drawing the graph $y = f(x)$ and finding where it crosses the line $y = k$.
> - trial and improvement.
> - rearranging the equation into the form $x = f(x)$ and solving by iteration (if the iterative formula converges).

Sometimes it can be worth using two methods: the graphical method to find how many solutions there are and then one of the other methods to find more precise solution(s).

Solve these equations by whichever method(s) you think suitable.

D1 Solve the equation $x^3 + 2x = 7$ to one decimal place.

D2 Find both solutions to the equation $x^2 - 2x = 3$.

D3 Find a number such that 7 times the number is equal to 1 plus its reciprocal.

D4 Find all the solutions to the equation $x^3 = 3x$.

D5 The formula for the area of a segment of a circle is $A = \frac{1}{2}r^2 (\phi - \sin \phi)$, where ϕ is the angle at the centre of the circle measured in radians.

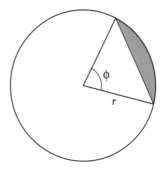

Find a value of ϕ which, for a 10 cm radius circle, will give a segment of area $100 \, \text{cm}^2$.

Find the angle in radians, then change it into degrees at the very end. (Remember π radians is 180°.)

D6 Solve the equation $\cos x = \frac{x}{3} - 1$ to 1 d.p.

D7 Find a value of x which satisfies $6 \cos x = 3$.

D8 One root of the equation $x^3 + px + q = 0$ is:

$$x = \sqrt[3]{\left(\frac{-q}{2} + \sqrt{\left(\frac{q^2}{4} + \frac{p^3}{27} \right)} \right)} - \sqrt[3]{\left(\frac{-q}{2} - \sqrt{\left(\frac{q^2}{4} + \frac{p^3}{27} \right)} \right)}$$

Use this formula or any other method to solve $x^3 - 3x + 4 = 0$. Give your answer correct to 2 d.p.

D9 Find an approximate solution to the equation $x^2 - 10x + 3 = 0$ to 3 d.p.

Summary

- Solving an equation by iteration involves rearranging it to give an iterative sequence of the form $u_{n+1} = f(u_n)$.

  For example, the equation $\quad x^2 = 2x + 2$
  rearranged is $\qquad\qquad\qquad x = \sqrt{(2x + 2)}$,
  giving the iterative formula $u_{n+1} = \sqrt{(2u_n + 2)}$.

  Taking $u_1 = 1$, the iterative sequence converges to a limit, which is a solution to the original equation $x^2 = 2x + 2$.

- Not all iterative sequences converge to a limit, so several rearrangements of the original equation may have to be tried. Whether the sequence converges or not may also depend on the value of u_1 chosen.

Mixed bag 3

1 Here are some figures showing the ages at death of some Egyptians whose mummies have been found.

Age at death	Male	Female	Age at death	Male	Female
1	2	1	28	0	1
2	2	0	29	1	1
3	3	2	30	1	2
4	4	3	31	0	0
5	3	0	32	1	0
6	0	2	33	2	1
7	1	0	35	0	3
8	0	0	36	2	2
9	0	1	37	1	0
10	1	1	40	3	3
11	1	1	46	1	0
12	0	0	48	2	0
13	0	0	50	5	1
14	2	1	52	3	1
15	0	0	54	0	1
16	1	1	55	2	1
17	2	3	59	1	0
18	0	2	60	4	1
19	1	2	62	1	0
20	2	3	63	1	0
21	1	6	65	2	0
22	2	2	68	2	0
23	1	2	70	1	1
24	2	0	72	3	1
25	5	4	84	1	0
26	4	1	90	1	0
27	1	1	96	0	1

How would you go about answering the question
'Do modern people live longer than Ancient Egyptians?'
Investigate the problem for yourself.

2 Investigate and try to *explain why* this works.

> Enter the year of birth of an adult you know into your calculator.
> Find the sine of this.
> (**Hint:** You may need to subtract multiples of 360° from the year.)
> Now find the inverse sine of the display.
> The result shows their age in 1980!

Try the trick for other birth years.

3 In about 1550 BC the Egyptians used an expression similar to $\left(d - \dfrac{d}{9}\right)^2$ to calculate the area of a circle diameter d.
What value for π does this imply?

4 Copy and complete this algebraic multiplication grid.

×	$(x + 1)$	$(x + 3)$	$(x + 5)$
$(x - 1)$		$x^2 + 2x - 3$	$x^2 + 4x - 5$
	$x^2 + 5x + 4$		$x^2 + 9x + 20$
	$x^2 - 4x - 5$	$x^2 - 2x - 15$	$x^2 - 25$

Make up some similar grids for yourself.
Is there a minimum number of cells which need to be filled in so that a puzzle like this may be solved?

5 What's wrong here?

$$a = b$$

(multiplying both sides by a) $\qquad a^2 = ab$

(subtracting b^2) $\qquad a^2 - b^2 = ab - b^2$

(factorising each side) $\qquad (a - b)(a + b) = b(a - b)$

(dividing each side by $(a - b)$) $\qquad a + b = b$

But if $a = b$ and $a = 1$ then $2 = 1$!

6 A bag contains one counter, known to be either red or blue.
A red counter is put into the bag. The bag is shaken and a counter taken out. This counter is red. What is the probability that the counter left in the bag is red?

7 This problem was first given in a 15th century French book.

A carpenter agreed to work for 2 francs for each day he actually works and to forfeit 3 francs for each day he does not work.
At the end of thirty days he has to pay out exactly the same amount as he receives.

How many days did he work?

8 (a) A planner has to link up five cities by motorway. No three of the cities are on a straight line. Each city must be linked directly to every other one. What is the least number of roads required?

(b) Roads may cross over each other by flyovers if needed.
Flyovers are difficult and expensive to build.
What is the least number of flyovers needed?

9 Is $x > \dfrac{1}{x}$ for all values of x? Investigate.

Review questions

1 Angles and circles 1

1.1 O marks the centre of each circle.
Find the size of the angles marked *a* and *b*.
Give a reason for each step in your working.

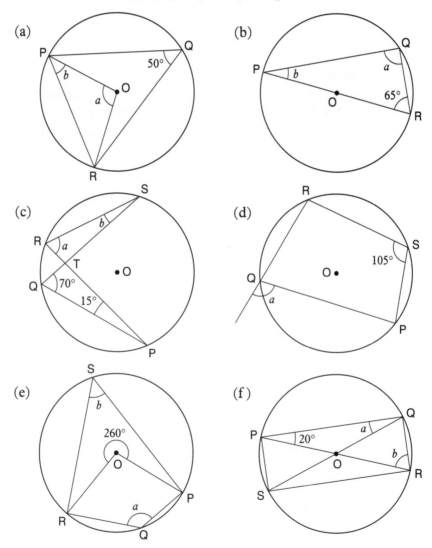

(a)

(b)

(c)

(d)

(e)

(f)

1.2 The points A, B, C and D are points, in order, on the circumference of a circle. ∠DAB is 120° and ∠CDA is 50°.
Find the sizes of ∠ABC and ∠DCB.

1.3 ABCD is a cyclic quadrilateral, $\angle ADC = 80°$, $\angle BCA = 30°$ and $\angle ACD = 60°$. Find the sizes of:

(a) $\angle DBA$ (b) $\angle DAB$ (c) $\angle DBC$ (d) $\angle ADB$

2   Rational and irrational numbers

2.1 Write these recurring decimals as fractions:

(a) $0\cdot1\dot{5}$ (b) $0\cdot3\dot{1}\dot{4}$ (c) $0\cdot\dot{2}$ (d) $0\cdot2\dot{8}\dot{4}$

2.2 Two numbers are called co-prime if they do not have any prime factors in common.

For example, 20 ($= 2 \times 2 \times 5$) and 21 ($= 3 \times 7$) are co-prime, but 20 ($= 2 \times 2 \times 5$) and 22 ($= 2 \times 11$) are not co-prime.

(a) Which of these pairs of numbers are co-prime? If they are not co-prime, give their common prime factor(s).

(i) 6 and 35   (ii) 18 and 19   (iii) 42 and 77   (iv) 36 and 108

(b) Investigate this statement: 'If the numbers a and b are co-prime and b and 10 are also co-prime, then the decimal equivalent of $\frac{a}{b}$ is recurring.'

(c) 'Pure' recurring decimals are those which begin repeating from the first digit. For example, $0\cdot\dot{1}71\dot{4}$ and $0\cdot\dot{2}\dot{7}$ are pure, but $0\cdot3\dot{2}1\dot{4}$ and $0\cdot73\dot{2}\dot{4}$ are not pure.

Do fractions of the form $\frac{1}{x}$, where x is co-prime with 10, always give a pure recurring decimal? Investigate.

2.3 'Any decimal can be written as a fraction.'
True or false? Explain your answer.

What about the reverse:
'Any fraction can be written as a decimal.'?

2.4 Investigate the last digit in the squares of whole numbers.

(a) Which digits occur?

(b) Which digits never occur in the last digit of $8a^2$, where a is a whole number?

(c) Use your answers to (a) and (b) to prove that $\sqrt{68}$ is irrational.

2.5 Which of these numbers are irrational?

(a) $\sqrt{16}$ (b) $\sqrt{18}$ (c) π (d) $0\cdot\dot{5}$

(e) $0\cdot110\,110\,011\,000\,110\,000\,11\ldots$

2.6 Find the values of each of these expressions.
State whether each one is rational or irrational.

(a) $(\sqrt{3} + 2) + (2 - \sqrt{3})$ (b) $(\sqrt{3} + 2)(2 - \sqrt{3})$ (c) $\sqrt{\frac{9}{16}}$

(d) $\sqrt{3}\,(\sqrt{12} + \sqrt{27})$ (e) $\sqrt{(2 + 14)}$ (f) $\sqrt{2} + \sqrt{14}$

2.7 Solve these equations. In each case say whether the solution is rational or not.

(a) $7x - 2 = 15$ (b) $2x - \sqrt{3} = \sqrt{6}$ (c) $\sqrt{(4x^2)} = 25$

(d) $x^2 - 1 = 3$ (e) $\sqrt{x} - 1 = 3$ (f) $x^2 - 1 = 2$

3 Tangents and curves

3.1 When large mirrors for telescopes are made, the glass must be cooled very slowly. Otherwise, the glass cools unevenly and may crack. To cool from 500 °C to 400 °C usually takes about 100 days.
What average cooling rate is this in °C/s (or °C s^{-1})?

3.2 A firework rocket is launched vertically. The table shows the distance above the ground as a function of time after launching.

Time (seconds)	0	0·5	1·0	1·5	2·0	2·5	3·0	3·5
Height (metres)	0	8·5	14·0	16·0	16·0	13·0	8·5	2·5

(a) Draw the graph of height against time for the rocket.

(b) Find the rocket's speed 1 second after launching.

(c) What is the maximum speed of the rocket?

(d) Estimate the speed at which the rocket hits the ground.

3.3 Describe what is happening to the acceleration of the car, from this velocity–time graph.

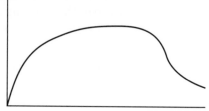

Velocity of car

Time

3.4 A parachutist is in free fall with a speed of 50 m/s.
She then opens her parachute.
This table gives her distance above the ground as a function of time after opening the parachute.

Time (seconds)	0	1	2	3	4	5	6	7	8	9	10	11	12	13
Height (metres)	200	187	176	168	161	154	148	143	138	132	127	122	117	112

(a) Draw this information on a graph.

(b) Find the velocity of the parachutist after falling for 2, 4, 6, 8, and 10 seconds after opening her parachute.

(c) Estimate how long it takes the parachutist to reach the ground.

(d) Use your results from (b) to draw another graph so that you can describe briefly how the acceleration changes as she descends.

4 Compounding errors

4.1 Calculate the upper and lower bounds (maximum and minimum values) for the following quantities.

(a) $40 \pm 2\,m^2$ (b) $58 \pm 0{\cdot}1°C$ (c) $671 \pm 0{\cdot}4\,km/hour$

4.2 Calculate the upper and lower bounds (maximum and minimum values) of the following quantities.

(a) $200\,km \pm 0{\cdot}5\%$ (b) $18\,km/hour \pm 5\%$

(c) $35\,ohms \pm 20\%$ (d) $10{\cdot}5\,seconds \pm 2\%$

4.3 Find the maximum and minimum possible volume of a cylinder of height $20 \pm 0{\cdot}5cm$ and diameter $10 \pm 0{\cdot}5\,cm$.

4.4 Find the least possible volume of a prism with area of cross-section $20\,cm^2 \pm 5\%$ and height $10 \pm 1\,cm$.

4.5 According to the *Fédération Internationale de l'Automobile* (FIA), which checks on all land speed records, to qualify for a new record a vehicle must exceed the existing record by $0{\cdot}001$ m.p.h. Speeds over the measured mile are now about 650 m.p.h.

How accurately must the measured mile and the time taken to cover it be measured to be accurate enough to distinguish speeds only $0{\cdot}001$ m.p.h. apart?

4.6 Cloud height, sometimes called cloud ceiling, may be found at night using this method. A searchlight a fixed distance d from the observation station is pointed directly upwards. At the observation post, the angle of elevation in degrees (e) of the point where the beam hits the cloud is measured. The cloud ceiling h is given by the formula: $h = d \tan e$.

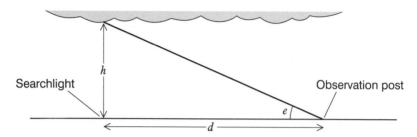

(a) What would be the relative error in cloud ceiling for these measurements: $e = 7 \pm 0.25°$ and $d = 1200\,\text{m} \pm 1\%$?

(b) In daytime a helium balloon is filled up so that it will just lift a standard weight. This standard weight is chosen so that the balloon will rise with a steady speed of 55 metres/minute. The time for the balloon to disappear in the cloud gives the cloud ceiling. The speed the balloon travels upwards has a relative uncertainty of about 5%. The time to disappear is accurate to ± 1 second.

For a cloud ceiling as in part (a), which method is more accurate – searchlight or helium balloon?

Give some figures to support your answer.

5 Using graphs to solve equations

5.1 Draw the graphs of $y = 4 \cos x$ and $y = \dfrac{x}{3}$ for $x = 0$ to 2π radians.

Use your graphs to solve these equations.
Give your answers to 1 decimal place.

(a) $4 \cos x = 0.5$ (b) $4 \cos x = \dfrac{x}{3}$ (c) $30 \cos x = \dfrac{5x}{2}$

5.2 There is a rough formula giving the playing time in minutes of tape in an old reel-to-reel tape recorder. If the thickness of tape is d inches, the playing time, t, in minutes is given by the formula:

$$t = 9.38(d^2 + 2.25d)$$

What thickness of tape will give a playing time of 30 minutes?

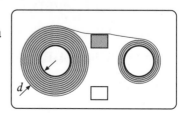

5.3 Use graphical methods to find both the roots of some quadratic equations of the form

$x^2 + x = c$, where c is a whole number.

Try to find a rule connecting the two roots with the value of c.

5.4 Draw the graph of $y = x^2 - 5x + 3$ and use it to solve these equations.

(a) $x^2 - 5x + 3 = x$ (b) $x^2 - 5x = 1$

5.5 Doctors are experimenting to find a formula which gives the number of people, n, who catch a contagious disease as a function of the time, t, in weeks since the beginning of the epidemic. A likely formula is:

$$n = \frac{1000t^2}{t^2 + 1}$$

According to the formula, after how many weeks will 500 people have caught the disease?

As time goes on, the number of people who have suffered from the disease gets closer to a certain number.

What do you think this number might represent?

5.6 A firefly is a type of beetle. It gets its name because it can produce flashing light by a chemical reaction in its body.

The brightness of the light fireflies emit is a function of temperature (for temperatures above freezing).

$I = {}^-0{\cdot}01t^3 + 0{\cdot}4t^2 + 0{\cdot}3t + 10,$

where I is the light intensity and t the temperature in °C.

(a) At about what temperature do the fireflies produce the brightest light?

(b) Find the two temperatures where the brightness is half this maximum value. Which is the more realistic temperature?

6 Congruency

6.1 In triangles ABC and DEF certain angles and sides are equal as given below. Say whether or not the triangles are necessarily congruent. If they are congruent, give the condition (SSS, etc.).

(a) $\angle CAB = \angle FDE$, AC = DF and AB = DE

(b) $\angle FDE = \angle FED$, $\angle CAB = \angle ACB$ and AC = DF

(c) $\angle CAB = \angle FDE$, AB = DE and CB = EF

(d) $\angle ABC = \angle DEF$, AC = DF and AB = DE

(e) $\angle ABC = \angle DEF$, $\angle CAB = \angle FDE$ and AB = DE

6.2 Two triangles have their corresponding angles equal.
The two triangles also have the same area.
Are the two triangles congruent? Explain your answer.

6.3 Prove that the diagonals of a rhombus bisect their angles.

6.4 ABC and DEF are acute-angled triangles, in which AB = DE,
AC = DF, and the perpendicular from A to BC is equal to the
perpendicular from D to EF.

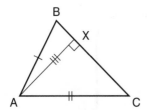 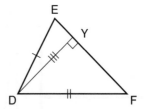

Prove that triangle ABC is congruent to triangle DEF.
Don't forget to give a reason for each step in your argument.

6.5 In triangle ABC, AD is the bisector of $\angle$BAC. From a point O on AD,
perpendiculars OE and OF are drawn to AB and AC. Prove that
OE = OF.

6.6 Here is a proof of Pythagoras' rule.
The triangle ABC has a right-angle at A.
AD is drawn perpendicular to BC and extended to E, where AE = BC.
From E draw EF perpendicular to AB and join E to B and C.

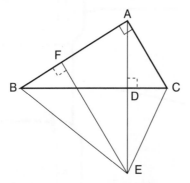

(a) Prove that triangles AFE and BAC are congruent.

(b) Use the result of part (a) and the fact that the area of ABEC is half
the product of the length of the diagonals to prove Pythagoras' rule
for triangle ABC.

7 Good fit?

7.1 Below are some graphs labelled A, B, C, D, E and F. Match as many expressions as you can with graphs.

(a) $y \propto x^2$

(b) $y = \sqrt{x} + 4$

(c) $y \propto \sqrt{x}$

(d) $y = \dfrac{x^3}{100} + 3$

(e) $y = \dfrac{x^2}{10}$

(f) $y = \dfrac{1}{x^2} + 5$

(g) $y \propto \dfrac{1}{x^2}$

(h) $y^2 \propto x$

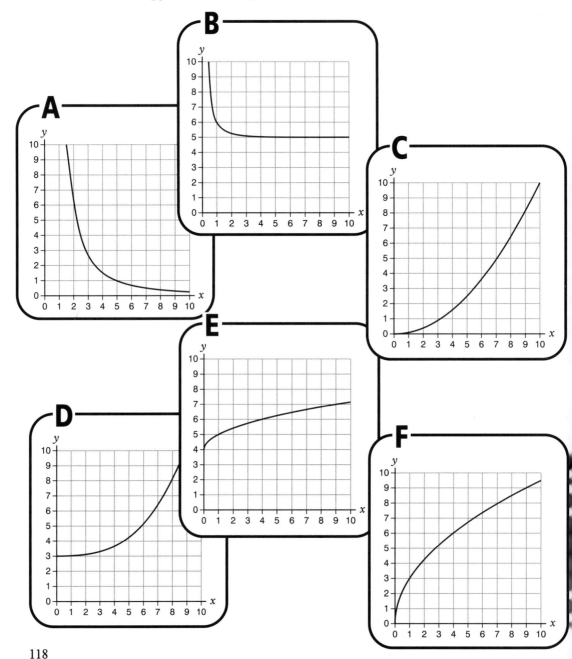

7.2 If $a \propto b$ and $b \propto c^2$, write down a relation connecting a and c.

Check your answer by changing the 'proportional to' to an equality.

7.3 How would you explain what each of these mean? Use examples to help you.

(a) $d \propto e^2$ (b) $e \propto \sqrt{f}$ (c) $y \propto \dfrac{1}{z^2}$

7.4 In an experiment a student put a 250 g load on the end of a wooden ruler.

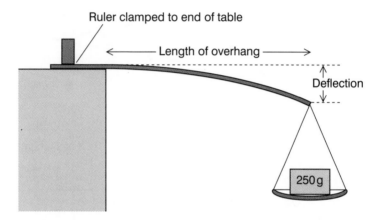

Ruler clamped to end of table

Length of overhang

Deflection

250 g

She then measured the deflection (dip) of this end as she varied the length of ruler overhanging the edge.

Here are her results.

Length of ruler overhang (cm)	20	30	40	50	60	70
Deflection (mm)	4	16	29	59	109	186

Janine says that the deflection is proportional to the overhang length squared. Abigail says it is proportional to this length cubed.

Show who is probably correct. Explain your answer carefully.

Find an empirical equation connecting the two lengths.

8 Angles and circles 2

8.1 O is the centre of each circle. Calculate the angles marked with letters. Don't forget to give a reason for each step in your working.

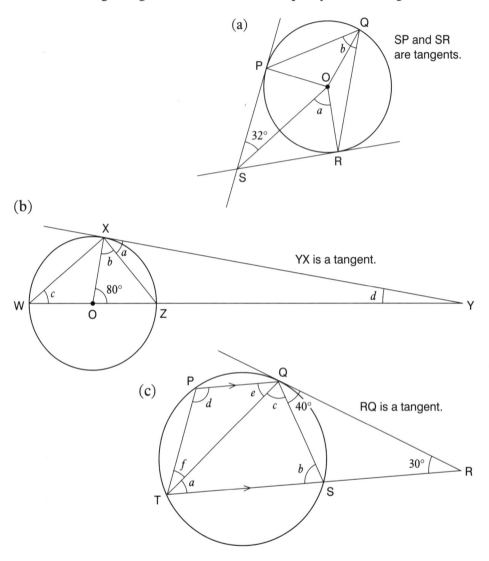

(a) SP and SR are tangents.

(b) YX is a tangent.

(c) RQ is a tangent.

8.2 CB and AB are tangents to the circle whose centre is O. The lines OA and BC are equal in length.

Explain why ABCO must be a square.

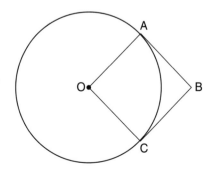

8.3 Here are two circles, with centres at X and Y.

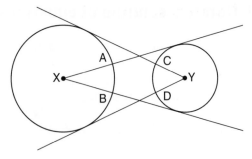

Tangents to each circle from the centre of the other are drawn.

Can you find, *by drawing*, a connection between the lengths of the chords AB and CD?

Does it depend on the distance between the two centres X and Y?

8.4 A, C and T are points on the circumference of a circle. AC is a diameter and TD is a tangent.

Explain what is wrong.

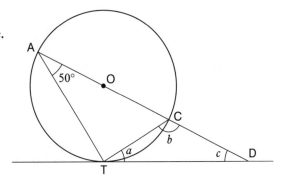

9 Introduction to matrices

9.1 Explain how to find the matrix product of the matrices:

$$\begin{bmatrix} 1 & 2 \\ 0 & 3 \end{bmatrix} \text{ and } \begin{bmatrix} 0 & 1 \\ 2 & 2 \end{bmatrix}$$

Does it matter in which order you work out the product?

9.2 A, B and C are three matrices,

$$\text{where } A = \begin{bmatrix} 3 & 0 \\ 0 & 1 \\ 2 & 1 \end{bmatrix}, \ B = \begin{bmatrix} 1 & -1 \\ 0 & 2 \end{bmatrix} \text{ and } C = \begin{bmatrix} -1 & 0 \\ 2 & 1 \end{bmatrix}$$

Write down the matrices represented by these. (If any are not possible, say so.)

   (a) 2B   (b) B + A   (c) BB   (d) AB

   (e) BC   (f) CB   (g) BA   (h) B – C

9.3 Write down two matrices whose products give a 3 × 2 matrix. Work out the product of your two matrices.

10 Iterative solution of equations

10.1 Calculate enough terms for each of these iterative formulas to convince yourself whether or not the sequence approaches (converges to) a limit, with the given value of the first term. If it does converge, write down the limit, correct to 2 decimal places.

(a) $u_{n+1} = \dfrac{2}{u_n} + 2$ $u_1 = 10$

(b) $u_{n+1} = \dfrac{10}{u_n}$ $u_1 = 2$

(c) $u_{n+1} = \dfrac{u_n^2 + 2}{5}$ $u_1 = 6$

(d) $u_{n+1} = \dfrac{u_n^2 + 2}{5}$ $u_1 = 4$

10.2 Use the iterative formula $u_{n+1} = \dfrac{5}{u_n + 2}$ with $u_1 = 1$
to find one solution to the quadratic equation $x^2 + 2x - 5 = 0$.
Give your solution correct to 2 decimal places.

10.3 Write down the quadratic equations which give rise to these iterative formulas.

(a) $u_{n+1} = \dfrac{10}{u_n}$ (b) $u_{n+1} = \dfrac{u_n^2 + 2}{5}$

(c) $u_{n+1} = \dfrac{2}{u_n} + 2$ (d) $u_{n+1} = \sqrt{(u_n + 3)}$

10.4 Write down an iterative formula (i.e. $x = f(x)$) which can be used to find a solution for each of these equations.

(a) $x^2 - 2x - 3 = 0$ (b) $x^2 - 3 = 0$

(c) $x^2 - 7x = 3$ (d) $x^2 = x + 4$

10.5 Write down an iterative formula for this equation.

$10x - 1 - \cos x = 0$

Use your iterative formula to solve the equation to 2 decimal places.
(**Hint:** Think about the units for x.)